Theodor W. Adorno: A Very Short Introduction

VERY SHORT INTRODUCTIONS are for anyone wanting a stimulating and accessible way into a new subject. They are written by experts, and have been translated into more than 45 different languages.

The series began in 1995, and now covers a wide variety of topics in every discipline. The VSI library currently contains over 700 volumes—a Very Short Introduction to everything from Psychology and Philosophy of Science to American History and Relativity—and continues to grow in every subject area.

Very Short Introductions available now:

ABOLITIONISM Richard S. Newman
THE ABRAHAMIC RELIGIONS
    Charles L. Cohen
ACCOUNTING Christopher Nobes
ADOLESCENCE Peter K. Smith
THEODOR W. ADORNO
    Andrew Bowie
ADVERTISING Winston Fletcher
AERIAL WARFARE Frank Ledwidge
AESTHETICS Bence Nanay
AFRICAN AMERICAN
    RELIGION Eddie S. Glaude Jr
AFRICAN HISTORY
    John Parker and Richard Rathbone
AFRICAN POLITICS Ian Taylor
AFRICAN RELIGIONS Jacob K. Olupona
AGEING Nancy A. Pachana
AGNOSTICISM Robin Le Poidevin
AGRICULTURE
    Paul Brassley and Richard Soffe
ALEXANDER THE GREAT
    Hugh Bowden
ALGEBRA Peter M. Higgins
AMERICAN BUSINESS HISTORY
    Walter A. Friedman
AMERICAN CULTURAL HISTORY
    Eric Avila
AMERICAN FOREIGN RELATIONS
    Andrew Preston
AMERICAN HISTORY Paul S. Boyer
AMERICAN IMMIGRATION
    David A. Gerber
AMERICAN INTELLECTUAL
    HISTORY
    Jennifer Ratner-Rosenhagen

AMERICAN LEGAL HISTORY
    G. Edward White
AMERICAN MILITARY HISTORY
    Joseph T. Glatthaar
AMERICAN NAVAL HISTORY
    Craig L. Symonds
AMERICAN POETRY David Caplan
AMERICAN POLITICAL
    HISTORY Donald Critchlow
AMERICAN POLITICAL PARTIES
    AND ELECTIONS L. Sandy Maisel
AMERICAN POLITICS
    Richard M. Valelly
THE AMERICAN PRESIDENCY
    Charles O. Jones
THE AMERICAN REVOLUTION
    Robert J. Allison
AMERICAN SLAVERY
    Heather Andrea Williams
THE AMERICAN SOUTH
    Charles Reagan Wilson
THE AMERICAN WEST
    Stephen Aron
AMERICAN WOMEN'S HISTORY
    Susan Ware
AMPHIBIANS T. S. Kemp
ANAESTHESIA Aidan O'Donnell
ANALYTIC PHILOSOPHY
    Michael Beaney
ANARCHISM Colin Ward
ANCIENT ASSYRIA Karen Radner
ANCIENT EGYPT Ian Shaw
ANCIENT EGYPTIAN ART AND
    ARCHITECTURE Christina Riggs
ANCIENT GREECE Paul Cartledge

THE ANCIENT NEAR EAST
Amanda H. Podany
ANCIENT PHILOSOPHY Julia Annas
ANCIENT WARFARE
Harry Sidebottom
ANGELS David Albert Jones
ANGLICANISM Mark Chapman
THE ANGLO-SAXON AGE John Blair
ANIMAL BEHAVIOUR
Tristram D. Wyatt
THE ANIMAL KINGDOM
Peter Holland
ANIMAL RIGHTS David DeGrazia
THE ANTARCTIC Klaus Dodds
ANTHROPOCENE Erle C. Ellis
ANTISEMITISM Steven Beller
ANXIETY Daniel Freeman and
Jason Freeman
THE APOCRYPHAL GOSPELS
Paul Foster
APPLIED MATHEMATICS
Alain Goriely
THOMAS AQUINAS Fergus Kerr
ARBITRATION Thomas Schultz and
Thomas Grant
ARCHAEOLOGY Paul Bahn
ARCHITECTURE Andrew Ballantyne
THE ARCTIC Klaus Dodds and
Jamie Woodward
ARISTOCRACY William Doyle
ARISTOTLE Jonathan Barnes
ART HISTORY Dana Arnold
ART THEORY Cynthia Freeland
ARTIFICIAL INTELLIGENCE
Margaret A. Boden
ASIAN AMERICAN HISTORY
Madeline Y. Hsu
ASTROBIOLOGY David C. Catling
ASTROPHYSICS James Binney
ATHEISM Julian Baggini
THE ATMOSPHERE Paul I. Palmer
AUGUSTINE Henry Chadwick
JANE AUSTEN Tom Keymer
AUSTRALIA Kenneth Morgan
AUTISM Uta Frith
AUTOBIOGRAPHY Laura Marcus
THE AVANT GARDE
David Cottington
THE AZTECS David Carrasco
BABYLONIA Trevor Bryce
BACTERIA Sebastian G. B. Amyes

BANKING John Goddard and
John O. S. Wilson
BARTHES Jonathan Culler
THE BEATS David Sterritt
BEAUTY Roger Scruton
BEHAVIOURAL ECONOMICS
Michelle Baddeley
BESTSELLERS John Sutherland
THE BIBLE John Riches
BIBLICAL ARCHAEOLOGY
Eric H. Cline
BIG DATA Dawn E. Holmes
BIOCHEMISTRY Mark Lorch
BIOGEOGRAPHY Mark V. Lomolino
BIOGRAPHY Hermione Lee
BIOMETRICS Michael Fairhurst
ELIZABETH BISHOP
Jonathan F. S. Post
BLACK HOLES Katherine Blundell
BLASPHEMY Yvonne Sherwood
BLOOD Chris Cooper
THE BLUES Elijah Wald
THE BODY Chris Shilling
THE BOOK OF COMMON PRAYER
Brian Cummings
THE BOOK OF MORMON
Terryl Givens
BORDERS Alexander C. Diener and
Joshua Hagen
THE BRAIN Michael O'Shea
BRANDING Robert Jones
THE BRICS Andrew F. Cooper
THE BRITISH CONSTITUTION
Martin Loughlin
THE BRITISH EMPIRE Ashley Jackson
BRITISH POLITICS Tony Wright
BUDDHA Michael Carrithers
BUDDHISM Damien Keown
BUDDHIST ETHICS Damien Keown
BYZANTIUM Peter Sarris
CALVINISM Jon Balserak
ALBERT CAMUS Oliver Gloag
CANADA Donald Wright
CANCER Nicholas James
CAPITALISM James Fulcher
CATHOLICISM Gerald O'Collins
CAUSATION Stephen Mumford and
Rani Lill Anjum
THE CELL Terence Allen and
Graham Cowling
THE CELTS Barry Cunliffe

CHAOS Leonard Smith
GEOFFREY CHAUCER David Wallace
CHEMISTRY Peter Atkins
CHILD PSYCHOLOGY Usha Goswami
CHILDREN'S LITERATURE
    Kimberley Reynolds
CHINESE LITERATURE Sabina Knight
CHOICE THEORY Michael Allingham
CHRISTIAN ART Beth Williamson
CHRISTIAN ETHICS D. Stephen Long
CHRISTIANITY Linda Woodhead
CIRCADIAN RHYTHMS
    Russell Foster and Leon Kreitzman
CITIZENSHIP Richard Bellamy
CITY PLANNING Carl Abbott
CIVIL ENGINEERING
    David Muir Wood
CLASSICAL LITERATURE William Allan
CLASSICAL MYTHOLOGY
    Helen Morales
CLASSICS
    Mary Beard and John Henderson
CLAUSEWITZ Michael Howard
CLIMATE Mark Maslin
CLIMATE CHANGE Mark Maslin
CLINICAL PSYCHOLOGY
    Susan Llewelyn and
    Katie Aafjes-van Doorn
COGNITIVE BEHAVIOURAL
    THERAPY Freda McManus
COGNITIVE NEUROSCIENCE
    Richard Passingham
THE COLD WAR Robert J. McMahon
COLONIAL AMERICA Alan Taylor
COLONIAL LATIN AMERICAN
    LITERATURE Rolena Adorno
COMBINATORICS Robin Wilson
COMEDY Matthew Bevis
COMMUNISM Leslie Holmes
COMPARATIVE LITERATURE
    Ben Hutchinson
COMPETITION AND ANTITRUST
    LAW Ariel Ezrachi
COMPLEXITY John H. Holland
THE COMPUTER Darrel Ince
COMPUTER SCIENCE
    Subrata Dasgupta
CONCENTRATION CAMPS
    Dan Stone
CONFUCIANISM Daniel K. Gardner

THE CONQUISTADORS
    Matthew Restall and
    Felipe Fernández-Armesto
CONSCIENCE Paul Strohm
CONSCIOUSNESS Susan Blackmore
CONTEMPORARY ART
    Julian Stallabrass
CONTEMPORARY FICTION
    Robert Eaglestone
CONTINENTAL PHILOSOPHY
    Simon Critchley
COPERNICUS Owen Gingerich
CORAL REEFS Charles Sheppard
CORPORATE SOCIAL
    RESPONSIBILITY Jeremy Moon
CORRUPTION Leslie Holmes
COSMOLOGY Peter Coles
COUNTRY MUSIC Richard Carlin
CREATIVITY Vlad Glăveanu
CRIME FICTION Richard Bradford
CRIMINAL JUSTICE Julian V. Roberts
CRIMINOLOGY Tim Newburn
CRITICAL THEORY
    Stephen Eric Bronner
THE CRUSADES Christopher Tyerman
CRYPTOGRAPHY Fred Piper and
    Sean Murphy
CRYSTALLOGRAPHY A. M. Glazer
THE CULTURAL REVOLUTION
    Richard Curt Kraus
DADA AND SURREALISM
    David Hopkins
DANTE Peter Hainsworth and
    David Robey
DARWIN Jonathan Howard
THE DEAD SEA SCROLLS
    Timothy H. Lim
DECADENCE David Weir
DECOLONIZATION
    Dane Kennedy
DEMENTIA Kathleen Taylor
DEMOCRACY Bernard Crick
DEMOGRAPHY Sarah Harper
DEPRESSION Jan Scott and
    Mary Jane Tacchi
DERRIDA Simon Glendinning
DESCARTES Tom Sorell
DESERTS Nick Middleton
DESIGN John Heskett
DEVELOPMENT Ian Goldin

DEVELOPMENTAL BIOLOGY
  Lewis Wolpert
THE DEVIL Darren Oldridge
DIASPORA Kevin Kenny
CHARLES DICKENS Jenny Hartley
DICTIONARIES Lynda Mugglestone
DINOSAURS David Norman
DIPLOMATIC HISTORY
  Joseph M. Siracusa
DOCUMENTARY FILM
  Patricia Aufderheide
DREAMING J. Allan Hobson
DRUGS Les Iversen
DRUIDS Barry Cunliffe
DYNASTY Jeroen Duindam
DYSLEXIA Margaret J. Snowling
EARLY MUSIC Thomas Forrest Kelly
THE EARTH Martin Redfern
EARTH SYSTEM SCIENCE Tim Lenton
ECOLOGY Jaboury Ghazoul
ECONOMICS Partha Dasgupta
EDUCATION Gary Thomas
EGYPTIAN MYTH Geraldine Pinch
EIGHTEENTH-CENTURY
  BRITAIN Paul Langford
THE ELEMENTS Philip Ball
EMOTION Dylan Evans
EMPIRE Stephen Howe
EMPLOYMENT LAW David Cabrelli
ENERGY SYSTEMS Nick Jenkins
ENGELS Terrell Carver
ENGINEERING David Blockley
THE ENGLISH LANGUAGE
  Simon Horobin
ENGLISH LITERATURE Jonathan Bate
THE ENLIGHTENMENT
  John Robertson
ENTREPRENEURSHIP
  Paul Westhead and Mike Wright
ENVIRONMENTAL
  ECONOMICS Stephen Smith
ENVIRONMENTAL ETHICS
  Robin Attfield
ENVIRONMENTAL LAW
  Elizabeth Fisher
ENVIRONMENTAL
  POLITICS Andrew Dobson
ENZYMES Paul Engel
EPICUREANISM Catherine Wilson
EPIDEMIOLOGY Rodolfo Saracci

ETHICS Simon Blackburn
ETHNOMUSICOLOGY Timothy Rice
THE ETRUSCANS Christopher Smith
EUGENICS Philippa Levine
THE EUROPEAN UNION
  Simon Usherwood and John Pinder
EUROPEAN UNION LAW
  Anthony Arnull
EVOLUTION Brian and
  Deborah Charlesworth
EXISTENTIALISM Thomas Flynn
EXPLORATION Stewart A. Weaver
EXTINCTION Paul B. Wignall
THE EYE Michael Land
FAIRY TALE Marina Warner
FAMILY LAW Jonathan Herring
MICHAEL FARADAY
  Frank A. J. L. James
FASCISM Kevin Passmore
FASHION Rebecca Arnold
FEDERALISM
  Mark J. Rozell and Clyde Wilcox
FEMINISM Margaret Walters
FILM Michael Wood
FILM MUSIC Kathryn Kalinak
FILM NOIR James Naremore
FIRE Andrew C. Scott
THE FIRST WORLD WAR
  Michael Howard
FOLK MUSIC Mark Slobin
FOOD John Krebs
FORENSIC PSYCHOLOGY
  David Canter
FORENSIC SCIENCE Jim Fraser
FORESTS Jaboury Ghazoul
FOSSILS Keith Thomson
FOUCAULT Gary Gutting
THE FOUNDING FATHERS
  R. B. Bernstein
FRACTALS Kenneth Falconer
FREE SPEECH Nigel Warburton
FREE WILL Thomas Pink
FREEMASONRY Andreas Önnerfors
FRENCH LITERATURE John D. Lyons
FRENCH PHILOSOPHY
  Stephen Gaukroger and Knox Peden
THE FRENCH REVOLUTION
  William Doyle
FREUD Anthony Storr
FUNDAMENTALISM Malise Ruthven

FUNGI Nicholas P. Money
THE FUTURE Jennifer M. Gidley
GALAXIES John Gribbin
GALILEO Stillman Drake
GAME THEORY Ken Binmore
GANDHI Bhikhu Parekh
GARDEN HISTORY Gordon Campbell
GENES Jonathan Slack
GENIUS Andrew Robinson
GENOMICS John Archibald
GEOGRAPHY John Matthews and
    David Herbert
GEOLOGY Jan Zalasiewicz
GEOMETRY Maciej Dunajski
GEOPHYSICS William Lowrie
GEOPOLITICS Klaus Dodds
GERMAN LITERATURE Nicholas Boyle
GERMAN PHILOSOPHY
    Andrew Bowie
THE GHETTO Bryan Cheyette
GLACIATION David J. A. Evans
GLOBAL CATASTROPHES Bill McGuire
GLOBAL ECONOMIC HISTORY
    Robert C. Allen
GLOBAL ISLAM Nile Green
GLOBALIZATION Manfred B. Steger
GOD John Bowker
GOETHE Ritchie Robertson
THE GOTHIC Nick Groom
GOVERNANCE Mark Bevir
GRAVITY Timothy Clifton
THE GREAT DEPRESSION AND
    THE NEW DEAL Eric Rauchway
HABEAS CORPUS Amanda Tyler
HABERMAS James Gordon Finlayson
THE HABSBURG EMPIRE
    Martyn Rady
HAPPINESS Daniel M. Haybron
THE HARLEM RENAISSANCE
    Cheryl A. Wall
THE HEBREW BIBLE AS LITERATURE
    Tod Linafelt
HEGEL Peter Singer
HEIDEGGER Michael Inwood
THE HELLENISTIC AGE
    Peter Thonemann
HEREDITY John Waller
HERMENEUTICS Jens Zimmermann
HERODOTUS Jennifer T. Roberts
HIEROGLYPHS Penelope Wilson

HINDUISM Kim Knott
HISTORY John H. Arnold
THE HISTORY OF ASTRONOMY
    Michael Hoskin
THE HISTORY OF CHEMISTRY
    William H. Brock
THE HISTORY OF CHILDHOOD
    James Marten
THE HISTORY OF CINEMA
    Geoffrey Nowell-Smith
THE HISTORY OF LIFE
    Michael Benton
THE HISTORY OF MATHEMATICS
    Jacqueline Stedall
THE HISTORY OF MEDICINE
    William Bynum
THE HISTORY OF PHYSICS
    J. L. Heilbron
THE HISTORY OF POLITICAL
    THOUGHT Richard Whatmore
THE HISTORY OF TIME
    Leofranc Holford-Strevens
HIV AND AIDS Alan Whiteside
HOBBES Richard Tuck
HOLLYWOOD Peter Decherney
THE HOLY ROMAN EMPIRE
    Joachim Whaley
HOME Michael Allen Fox
HOMER Barbara Graziosi
HORMONES Martin Luck
HORROR Darryl Jones
HUMAN ANATOMY
    Leslie Klenerman
HUMAN EVOLUTION Bernard Wood
HUMAN PHYSIOLOGY
    Jamie A. Davies
HUMAN RESOURCE
    MANAGEMENT Adrian Wilkinson
HUMAN RIGHTS Andrew Clapham
HUMANISM Stephen Law
HUME James A. Harris
HUMOUR Noël Carroll
THE ICE AGE Jamie Woodward
IDENTITY Florian Coulmas
IDEOLOGY Michael Freeden
THE IMMUNE SYSTEM
    Paul Klenerman
INDIAN CINEMA
    Ashish Rajadhyaksha
INDIAN PHILOSOPHY Sue Hamilton

THE INDUSTRIAL REVOLUTION
Robert C. Allen
INFECTIOUS DISEASE Marta L. Wayne
and Benjamin M. Bolker
INFINITY Ian Stewart
INFORMATION Luciano Floridi
INNOVATION
Mark Dodgson and David Gann
INTELLECTUAL PROPERTY
Siva Vaidhyanathan
INTELLIGENCE Ian J. Deary
INTERNATIONAL LAW
Vaughan Lowe
INTERNATIONAL MIGRATION
Khalid Koser
INTERNATIONAL RELATIONS
Christian Reus-Smit
INTERNATIONAL SECURITY
Christopher S. Browning
IRAN Ali M. Ansari
ISLAM Malise Ruthven
ISLAMIC HISTORY Adam Silverstein
ISLAMIC LAW Mashood A. Baderin
ISOTOPES Rob Ellam
ITALIAN LITERATURE
Peter Hainsworth and David Robey
HENRY JAMES Susan L. Mizruchi
JESUS Richard Bauckham
JEWISH HISTORY David N. Myers
JEWISH LITERATURE Ilan Stavans
JOURNALISM Ian Hargreaves
JAMES JOYCE Colin MacCabe
JUDAISM Norman Solomon
JUNG Anthony Stevens
KABBALAH Joseph Dan
KAFKA Ritchie Robertson
KANT Roger Scruton
KEYNES Robert Skidelsky
KIERKEGAARD Patrick Gardiner
KNOWLEDGE Jennifer Nagel
THE KORAN Michael Cook
KOREA Michael J. Seth
LAKES Warwick F. Vincent
LANDSCAPE ARCHITECTURE
Ian H. Thompson
LANDSCAPES AND
GEOMORPHOLOGY
Andrew Goudie and Heather Viles
LANGUAGES Stephen R. Anderson
LATE ANTIQUITY Gillian Clark

LAW Raymond Wacks
THE LAWS OF THERMODYNAMICS
Peter Atkins
LEADERSHIP Keith Grint
LEARNING Mark Haselgrove
LEIBNIZ Maria Rosa Antognazza
C. S. LEWIS James Como
LIBERALISM Michael Freeden
LIGHT Ian Walmsley
LINCOLN Allen C. Guelzo
LINGUISTICS Peter Matthews
LITERARY THEORY Jonathan Culler
LOCKE John Dunn
LOGIC Graham Priest
LOVE Ronald de Sousa
MARTIN LUTHER Scott H. Hendrix
MACHIAVELLI Quentin Skinner
MADNESS Andrew Scull
MAGIC Owen Davies
MAGNA CARTA Nicholas Vincent
MAGNETISM Stephen Blundell
MALTHUS Donald Winch
MAMMALS T. S. Kemp
MANAGEMENT John Hendry
NELSON MANDELA Elleke Boehmer
MAO Delia Davin
MARINE BIOLOGY Philip V. Mladenov
MARKETING
Kenneth Le Meunier-FitzHugh
THE MARQUIS DE SADE
John Phillips
MARTYRDOM Jolyon Mitchell
MARX Peter Singer
MATERIALS Christopher Hall
MATHEMATICAL FINANCE
Mark H. A. Davis
MATHEMATICS Timothy Gowers
MATTER Geoff Cottrell
THE MAYA Matthew Restall and
Amara Solari
THE MEANING OF LIFE
Terry Eagleton
MEASUREMENT David Hand
MEDICAL ETHICS Michael Dunn and
Tony Hope
MEDICAL LAW Charles Foster
MEDIEVAL BRITAIN John Gillingham
and Ralph A. Griffiths
MEDIEVAL LITERATURE
Elaine Treharne

MEDIEVAL PHILOSOPHY
  John Marenbon
MEMORY Jonathan K. Foster
METAPHYSICS Stephen Mumford
METHODISM William J. Abraham
THE MEXICAN REVOLUTION
  Alan Knight
MICROBIOLOGY Nicholas P. Money
MICROECONOMICS Avinash Dixit
MICROSCOPY Terence Allen
THE MIDDLE AGES Miri Rubin
MILITARY JUSTICE Eugene R. Fidell
MILITARY STRATEGY
  Antulio J. Echevarria II
JOHN STUART MILL Gregory Claeys
MINERALS David Vaughan
MIRACLES Yujin Nagasawa
MODERN ARCHITECTURE
  Adam Sharr
MODERN ART David Cottington
MODERN BRAZIL Anthony W. Pereira
MODERN CHINA Rana Mitter
MODERN DRAMA
  Kirsten E. Shepherd-Barr
MODERN FRANCE
  Vanessa R. Schwartz
MODERN INDIA Craig Jeffrey
MODERN IRELAND Senia Pašeta
MODERN ITALY Anna Cento Bull
MODERN JAPAN
  Christopher Goto-Jones
MODERN LATIN AMERICAN
  LITERATURE
  Roberto González Echevarría
MODERN WAR Richard English
MODERNISM Christopher Butler
MOLECULAR BIOLOGY Aysha Divan
  and Janice A. Royds
MOLECULES Philip Ball
MONASTICISM Stephen J. Davis
THE MONGOLS Morris Rossabi
MONTAIGNE William M. Hamlin
MOONS David A. Rothery
MORMONISM Richard Lyman Bushman
MOUNTAINS Martin F. Price
MUHAMMAD Jonathan A. C. Brown
MULTICULTURALISM Ali Rattansi
MULTILINGUALISM John C. Maher
MUSIC Nicholas Cook
MYTH Robert A. Segal

NAPOLEON David Bell
THE NAPOLEONIC WARS
  Mike Rapport
NATIONALISM Steven Grosby
NATIVE AMERICAN LITERATURE
  Sean Teuton
NAVIGATION Jim Bennett
NAZI GERMANY Jane Caplan
NEOLIBERALISM Manfred B. Steger
  and Ravi K. Roy
NETWORKS Guido Caldarelli and
  Michele Catanzaro
THE NEW TESTAMENT
  Luke Timothy Johnson
THE NEW TESTAMENT AS
  LITERATURE Kyle Keefer
NEWTON Robert Iliffe
NIELS BOHR J. L. Heilbron
NIETZSCHE Michael Tanner
NINETEENTH-CENTURY BRITAIN
  Christopher Harvie and
  H. C. G. Matthew
THE NORMAN CONQUEST
  George Garnett
NORTH AMERICAN INDIANS
  Theda Perdue and Michael D. Green
NORTHERN IRELAND
  Marc Mulholland
NOTHING Frank Close
NUCLEAR PHYSICS Frank Close
NUCLEAR POWER Maxwell Irvine
NUCLEAR WEAPONS
  Joseph M. Siracusa
NUMBER THEORY Robin Wilson
NUMBERS Peter M. Higgins
NUTRITION David A. Bender
OBJECTIVITY Stephen Gaukroger
OCEANS Dorrik Stow
THE OLD TESTAMENT
  Michael D. Coogan
THE ORCHESTRA D. Kern Holoman
ORGANIC CHEMISTRY
  Graham Patrick
ORGANIZATIONS Mary Jo Hatch
ORGANIZED CRIME
  Georgios A. Antonopoulos and
  Georgios Papanicolaou
ORTHODOX CHRISTIANITY
  A. Edward Siecienski
OVID Llewelyn Morgan

PAGANISM Owen Davies
PAKISTAN Pippa Virdee
THE PALESTINIAN-ISRAELI
    CONFLICT Martin Bunton
PANDEMICS Christian W. McMillen
PARTICLE PHYSICS Frank Close
PAUL E. P. Sanders
PEACE Oliver P. Richmond
PENTECOSTALISM William K. Kay
PERCEPTION Brian Rogers
THE PERIODIC TABLE Eric R. Scerri
PHILOSOPHICAL METHOD
    Timothy Williamson
PHILOSOPHY Edward Craig
PHILOSOPHY IN THE ISLAMIC
    WORLD Peter Adamson
PHILOSOPHY OF BIOLOGY
    Samir Okasha
PHILOSOPHY OF LAW
    Raymond Wacks
PHILOSOPHY OF MIND
    Barbara Gail Montero
PHILOSOPHY OF PHYSICS
    David Wallace
PHILOSOPHY OF SCIENCE
    Samir Okasha
PHILOSOPHY OF RELIGION
    Tim Bayne
PHOTOGRAPHY Steve Edwards
PHYSICAL CHEMISTRY Peter Atkins
PHYSICS Sidney Perkowitz
PILGRIMAGE Ian Reader
PLAGUE Paul Slack
PLANETARY SYSTEMS
    Raymond T. Pierrehumbert
PLANETS David A. Rothery
PLANTS Timothy Walker
PLATE TECTONICS Peter Molnar
PLATO Julia Annas
POETRY Bernard O'Donoghue
POLITICAL PHILOSOPHY David Miller
POLITICS Kenneth Minogue
POLYGAMY Sarah M. S. Pearsall
POPULISM Cas Mudde and
    Cristóbal Rovira Kaltwasser
POSTCOLONIALISM Robert Young
POSTMODERNISM Christopher Butler
POSTSTRUCTURALISM
    Catherine Belsey
POVERTY Philip N. Jefferson

PREHISTORY Chris Gosden
PRESOCRATIC PHILOSOPHY
    Catherine Osborne
PRIVACY Raymond Wacks
PROBABILITY John Haigh
PROGRESSIVISM Walter Nugent
PROHIBITION W. J. Rorabaugh
PROJECTS Andrew Davies
PROTESTANTISM Mark A. Noll
PSYCHIATRY Tom Burns
PSYCHOANALYSIS Daniel Pick
PSYCHOLOGY
    Gillian Butler and Freda McManus
PSYCHOLOGY OF MUSIC
    Elizabeth Hellmuth Margulis
PSYCHOPATHY Essi Viding
PSYCHOTHERAPY
    Tom Burns and Eva Burns-Lundgren
PUBLIC ADMINISTRATION
    Stella Z. Theodoulou and Ravi K. Roy
PUBLIC HEALTH Virginia Berridge
PURITANISM Francis J. Bremer
THE QUAKERS Pink Dandelion
QUANTUM THEORY
    John Polkinghorne
RACISM Ali Rattansi
RADIOACTIVITY Claudio Tuniz
RASTAFARI Ennis B. Edmonds
READING Belinda Jack
THE REAGAN REVOLUTION Gil Troy
REALITY Jan Westerhoff
RECONSTRUCTION Allen C. Guelzo
THE REFORMATION Peter Marshall
REFUGEES Gil Loescher
RELATIVITY Russell Stannard
RELIGION Thomas A. Tweed
RELIGION IN AMERICA Timothy Beal
THE RENAISSANCE Jerry Brotton
RENAISSANCE ART
    Geraldine A. Johnson
RENEWABLE ENERGY Nick Jelley
REPTILES T.S. Kemp
REVOLUTIONS Jack A. Goldstone
RHETORIC Richard Toye
RISK Baruch Fischhoff and John Kadvany
RITUAL Barry Stephenson
RIVERS Nick Middleton
ROBOTICS Alan Winfield
ROCKS Jan Zalasiewicz
ROMAN BRITAIN Peter Salway

THE ROMAN EMPIRE
    Christopher Kelly
THE ROMAN REPUBLIC
    David M. Gwynn
ROMANTICISM Michael Ferber
ROUSSEAU Robert Wokler
RUSSELL A. C. Grayling
THE RUSSIAN ECONOMY
    Richard Connolly
RUSSIAN HISTORY Geoffrey Hosking
RUSSIAN LITERATURE Catriona Kelly
THE RUSSIAN REVOLUTION
    S. A. Smith
SAINTS Simon Yarrow
SAMURAI Michael Wert
SAVANNAS Peter A. Furley
SCEPTICISM Duncan Pritchard
SCHIZOPHRENIA
    Chris Frith and Eve Johnstone
SCHOPENHAUER
    Christopher Janaway
SCIENCE AND RELIGION Thomas
    Dixon and Adam R. Shapiro
SCIENCE FICTION David Seed
THE SCIENTIFIC REVOLUTION
    Lawrence M. Principe
SCOTLAND Rab Houston
SECULARISM Andrew Copson
SEXUAL SELECTION
    Marlene Zuk and Leigh W. Simmons
SEXUALITY Véronique Mottier
WILLIAM SHAKESPEARE
    Stanley Wells
SHAKESPEARE'S COMEDIES
    Bart van Es
SHAKESPEARE'S SONNETS AND
    POEMS Jonathan F. S. Post
SHAKESPEARE'S TRAGEDIES
    Stanley Wells
GEORGE BERNARD SHAW
    Christopher Wixson
MARY SHELLEY Charlotte Gordon
THE SHORT STORY Andrew Kahn
SIKHISM Eleanor Nesbitt
SILENT FILM Donna Kornhaber
THE SILK ROAD James A. Millward
SLANG Jonathon Green
SLEEP Steven W. Lockley and
    Russell G. Foster
SMELL Matthew Cobb

ADAM SMITH Christopher J. Berry
SOCIAL AND CULTURAL
    ANTHROPOLOGY
    John Monaghan and Peter Just
SOCIAL PSYCHOLOGY Richard J. Crisp
SOCIAL WORK Sally Holland and
    Jonathan Scourfield
SOCIALISM Michael Newman
SOCIOLINGUISTICS John Edwards
SOCIOLOGY Steve Bruce
SOCRATES C. C. W. Taylor
SOFT MATTER Tom McLeish
SOUND Mike Goldsmith
SOUTHEAST ASIA James R. Rush
THE SOVIET UNION Stephen Lovell
THE SPANISH CIVIL WAR
    Helen Graham
SPANISH LITERATURE Jo Labanyi
SPINOZA Roger Scruton
SPIRITUALITY Philip Sheldrake
SPORT Mike Cronin
STARS Andrew King
STATISTICS David J. Hand
STEM CELLS Jonathan Slack
STOICISM Brad Inwood
STRUCTURAL ENGINEERING
    David Blockley
STUART BRITAIN John Morrill
THE SUN Philip Judge
SUPERCONDUCTIVITY
    Stephen Blundell
SUPERSTITION Stuart Vyse
SYMMETRY Ian Stewart
SYNAESTHESIA Julia Simner
SYNTHETIC BIOLOGY Jamie A. Davies
SYSTEMS BIOLOGY Eberhard O. Voit
TAXATION Stephen Smith
TEETH Peter S. Ungar
TELESCOPES Geoff Cottrell
TERRORISM Charles Townshend
THEATRE Marvin Carlson
THEOLOGY David F. Ford
THINKING AND REASONING
    Jonathan St B. T. Evans
THOUGHT Tim Bayne
TIBETAN BUDDHISM
    Matthew T. Kapstein
TIDES David George Bowers and
    Emyr Martyn Roberts
TIME Jenann Ismael

TOCQUEVILLE Harvey C. Mansfield
LEO TOLSTOY Liza Knapp
TOPOLOGY Richard Earl
TRAGEDY Adrian Poole
TRANSLATION Matthew Reynolds
THE TREATY OF VERSAILLES
    Michael S. Neiberg
TRIGONOMETRY
    Glen Van Brummelen
THE TROJAN WAR Eric H. Cline
TRUST Katherine Hawley
THE TUDORS John Guy
TWENTIETH-CENTURY BRITAIN
    Kenneth O. Morgan
TYPOGRAPHY Paul Luna
THE UNITED NATIONS
    Jussi M. Hanhimäki
UNIVERSITIES AND COLLEGES
    David Palfreyman and Paul Temple
THE U.S. CIVIL WAR Louis P. Masur
THE U.S. CONGRESS
    Donald A. Ritchie
THE U.S. CONSTITUTION
    David J. Bodenhamer
THE U.S. SUPREME COURT
    Linda Greenhouse
UTILITARIANISM
    Katarzyna de Lazari-Radek and
    Peter Singer
UTOPIANISM Lyman Tower Sargent

VETERINARY SCIENCE James Yeates
THE VIKINGS Julian D. Richards
VIOLENCE Philip Dwyer
THE VIRGIN MARY
    Mary Joan Winn Leith
THE VIRTUES Craig A. Boyd and
    Kevin Timpe
VIRUSES Dorothy H. Crawford
VOLCANOES Michael J. Branney and
    Jan Zalasiewicz
VOLTAIRE Nicholas Cronk
WAR AND RELIGION
    Jolyon Mitchell and Joshua Rey
WAR AND TECHNOLOGY
    Alex Roland
WATER John Finney
WAVES Mike Goldsmith
WEATHER Storm Dunlop
THE WELFARE STATE David Garland
WITCHCRAFT Malcolm Gaskill
WITTGENSTEIN A. C. Grayling
WORK Stephen Fineman
WORLD MUSIC Philip Bohlman
THE WORLD TRADE
    ORGANIZATION Amrita Narlikar
WORLD WAR II Gerhard L. Weinberg
WRITING AND SCRIPT
    Andrew Robinson
ZIONISM Michael Stanislawski
ÉMILE ZOLA Brian Nelson

Available soon:

FLUID MECHANICS Eric Lauga
THE SPARTANS
    Andrew Bayliss

COGNITIVE BEHAVIOURAL
    THERAPY Freda McManus
EMPLOYMENT LAW David Cabrelli

For more information visit our website

www.oup.com/vsi/

Andrew Bowie

THEODOR
W. ADORNO

A Very Short Introduction

OXFORD
UNIVERSITY PRESS

Great Clarendon Street, Oxford, OX2 6DP,
United Kingdom

Oxford University Press is a department of the University of Oxford.
It furthers the University's objective of excellence in research, scholarship,
and education by publishing worldwide. Oxford is a registered trade mark of
Oxford University Press in the UK and in certain other countries

Published in the United States of America by Oxford University Press
198 Madison Avenue, New York, NY 10016, United States of America

British Library Cataloguing in Publication Data

Data available

Library of Congress Control Number: 2021949099

ISBN 978-0-19-883386-4

Printed in Great Britain by
Ashford Colour Press Ltd, Gosport, Hampshire

Contents

List of illustrations xvii

1 Life and times 1

2 The modern subject 11

3 Nature and history 27

4 History and freedom 38

5 The culture industry 53

6 Society 65

7 Art and philosophy 85

8 Doing justice to things 105

References 113

Further reading 119

Index 125

List of illustrations

1   Adorno with leaders of the Student Movement **9**
© Barbara Klemm

2   Horkheimer and Adorno **15**
Jeremy J. Shapiro/Wikipedia

3   Marx and Engels **32**
Mars 2002/Wikipedia

4   Hollywood **56**
colaimages/Alamy Stock Photo

5   Adorno **63**

6   Auschwitz I Main Camp **80**
National Archives, College Park, MD, courtesy of USHMM Photo Archives/Wikipedia

7   Paul Klee, *Death for the Idea* **103**
© 2021. Digital image, The Museum of Modern Art, New York/Scala, Florence

8   Adorno memorial in Frankfurt am Main **111**

Chapter 1
Life and times

Three months before philosopher and social and cultural theorist
T. W. Adorno's death in August 1969, an interview with him in the
German news magazine *Der Spiegel* opened with the following
exchange:

> Spiegel: 'Herr Professor, two weeks ago everything seemed alright
> with the world...'
>
> Adorno: 'Not to me it didn't.' (GS 20.1 p. 402)

Adorno's laconic response chimes with his search for answers, in
the wake of the Holocaust, to why the ever-increasing capacity for
knowledge and technological control of nature has not led to a
more humane world. Why, though, should a thinker notorious for
the complexity of his thought, and sometimes unnecessary
obscurity of his prose style, whose greatest interest was probably
Western 'classical' music, now be generating widespread
attention? The financial crisis that began in 2007, awareness of
the climate emergency, and the revival of fascism in some
countries have meant that, after a time in the 1980s and 1990s
when he rather faded from view, Adorno's insights into the ills of
the contemporary world seem ever more prescient. The prevailing
norms in much of economics, politics, and the social sciences in
the Thatcher–Reagan era, for which 'free-market', 'neoliberal'

capitalism is the only way to organize modern societies, have been increasingly discredited. Massive increases in wealth inequality, and the effects on the environment of underregulated markets and predatory transnational corporations have led to the point where the very survival of civilized human life on earth is in question. Given the failure of authoritarian communist regimes to offer a defensible alternative, Adorno's attempts to understand why the goal of a just political, economic, and social order has proved to be so elusive seem more and more relevant.

In a lecture on 'Aspects of the New Right-Wing Radicalism' of 1967 Adorno talks of a 'constellation of rational means and irrational purposes' in right-wing radicalism's often successful use of propaganda. He adds that this 'in a certain respect corresponds to the overall civilisational trend, that, after all, culminates in such a perfection of techniques and means, while the purpose of this for society as a whole goes by the board'. The core of Adorno's thinking is, then, in one sense quite simple: he asks why instead of everyone being fed, clothed, housed, and living a tolerable life, we are faced with mass poverty, enduring conflict, and the devastation of the natural world. So what does Adorno propose as a response to this situation?

Asked in the *Spiegel* interview about how his theoretical work can affect political practice, he insists: 'I try to express what I recognize and what I think. But I can't arrange this in terms of what one can do with it and what becomes of it' (GS 20.1 p. 403). Accused of therefore living in an ivory tower, he counters: 'I believe that a theory is more capable of being practically effective by dint of its own objectivity than if it subordinates itself to practice from the word go' (GS 20.1 p. 403)—elsewhere he says 'the demand for the unity of theory and praxis very easily leads to a kind of censorship of theory by praxis' (GS 8 p. 579). One reason for his saying this is that he thought the Student Movement of the late 1960s in Germany was pursuing unrealistic goals, and acted in sometimes violent ways, which could be seen as echoing the

Nazi past, and which hindered its emancipatory aims. His further reason is that the modern world renders decisions about what courses of action are justified ever more precarious. As he says in the collection of brief critical essays and aphorisms on modern culture, *Minima Moralia* (1951, but written during the war): 'The signature of the age is that, without exception, no person can themself determine their life in a half-way transparent sense, of the kind that used to be given in the appraisal of the state of the market' (GS 4 p. 41).

Although he rejects communism, Adorno still adheres in important respects to Marx's 'historical materialist' idea that how things are produced and exchanged influences people's thoughts and actions in ways which are not transparent to them. The search for objectivity is therefore conducted in circumstances where social and economic pressures make claims to objectivity inherently open to question: 'The almost insoluble task consists in not letting oneself be made stupid either by the power of others or by one's own powerlessness' (GS 4 p. 63). He consequently talks in 'Einleitung in die Philosophie' of philosophy as 'the comprehensive obligation not to be naïve'. The lesson of 20th-century history is that any modern society has the potential to fall into fascism and authoritarianism, because of its inherent economic instability and the conformist pressures it exerts on its members.

Adorno's life spanned the major upheavals of the 20th century. He was born in Frankfurt am Main, in 1903, in a mixed Jewish and Catholic family, as Theodor Wiesengrund Adorno. He was a precocious musical talent, began lessons in composition at the age of 16, and by the age of 18 was studying philosophy, music, and psychology at university, and publishing music criticism. He completed a PhD on the phenomenology of Edmund Husserl in 1924, and moved to Vienna in 1925 to study composition with Alban Berg. After returning to Frankfurt, while editing the musical journal *Anbruch* ('Dawn'), Adorno read Hungarian

Marxist philosopher and critic, Georg Lukács's, *History and Class-Consciousness*. He also developed intensive contact with cultural critic and philosopher Walter Benjamin, whom he had got to know in 1923. One of Benjamin's key ideas is that the truth provided by the mathematically based natural sciences is not the truth which should concern philosophy, and this leads him, and Adorno, to an enduring concern with art's relationship to philosophy. In 1931 Adorno finished his *Habilitation* (the German postdoctoral dissertation), *Kierkegaard: Construction of the Aesthetic* (which was heavily influenced by Benjamin), an analysis of Kierkegaard's concern with 'inwardness', in order to reveal the underlying repressive nature of bourgeois society. Adorno underestimated the dangers of the seizure of power by the Nazis, and continued to visit Germany until 1937, while an 'advanced student' at Merton College, Oxford. In 1938 he moved to the USA to work with Max Horkheimer, as a member of the Institute for Social Research, which had been exiled from Germany, living in New York, and then Los Angeles for the years 1941–9. During this period he wrote *Dialectic of Enlightenment* with Horkheimer, which consists of reflections on how modern rationality can turn into barbarism, *Minima Moralia*, *Philosophy of New Music*, which contrasts Schoenberg and Stravinsky as keys to the significance of modern music, and was a co-author of *The Authoritarian Personality*, which was part of the Berkeley 'Project on the Nature and Extent of Antisemitism'. Adorno returned to Frankfurt in 1949, where he gained his first (and only) tenured professorship, at the re-established Institute for Social Research, in 1956. In the early 1960s he was involved in the 'Positivism Dispute in German Sociology', a debate about theory and evidence in the social sciences, in which his main opponents were philosophers Karl Popper and Hans Albert. Throughout the 1960s he worked on his major texts on philosophy and aesthetics, *Negative Dialectics* and *Aesthetic Theory*, and other projects, while being active in public life in relation to the protests of the Student Movement and other social, political, and cultural issues. He died of a heart attack while on holiday in Switzerland in 1969.

Theodor W. Adorno

Adorno seems to have sometimes been quite a difficult character, but he also inspired great affection. The aim of the present introduction is to show the significance of his work for a contemporary audience, rather than using details about his life and character to interpret that work. His main works are written in a manner which deliberately resists summary, in order to avoid oversimplification of issues that need to be grasped in their complexity. Sometimes, though, this tips over into unnecessary opacity—his lectures, many of which have now been published, often deal with the same issues in a more lucid manner. Instead of summarizing Adorno's main works, I want, then, to delineate his key concerns that recur in a wide variety of texts, and will try as much as possible to let Adorno speak in his own words, as paraphrasing him can obscure key nuances.

Adorno's major concern can be seen in terms of understanding a world whose history often seemed to defy understanding. The history in question has been referred to by Eric Hobsbawm as the 'short 20th century', which begins with the outbreak of the First World War in 1914, and ends with the collapse of the Soviet Union in 1991. A key factor in what made the First World War possible, and had enduring negative consequences for the democratic Left, was the failure of the socialist parties of the Second International to put the interests of the European working class above national interests when war threatened. Among other things, this failure negatively influenced the course and effects of the Russian revolution. The War led to the break-up of the Austro-Hungarian, German, Ottoman, and Russian empires, and to ongoing political, social, and economic instability that eventually led to the Second World War and the unthinkable trauma of the Holocaust. International instability diminished somewhat with the conclusion of the Second World War in 1945, inaugurating a spell of growing economic prosperity in the West, despite the political tensions of the Cold War and the threat of atomic warfare. After Adorno's death, the oil crisis of 1973 undermined the foundations of this prosperity and allowed the political right, led by Ronald

Reagan and Margaret Thatcher, to begin to roll back some of the social and economic advances made in the preceding period. The collapse of Communism in Eastern Europe, instead of leading to further stabilization, led to new instability, involving, in the wake of the 2007 economic crash, a revival of authoritarian right-wing politics in the USA and parts of Europe and elsewhere that is thoroughly in line with Adorno's warnings after the war.

The political and economic upheavals of Adorno's world were accompanied by rapid and often disorienting changes in the arts, philosophy, and the sciences, and exploration of the relationships between these changes is central to his work. Weimar Germany and post-imperial Austria saw some of the most innovative and influential cultural responses to the disintegration of many of the structures and expectations of Western society and culture. Sigmund Freud's claims regarding the nature of the human mind, summarized in his dictum that the I is not 'lord in its own house', because its real motivations are often hidden in the unconscious, Max Weber's analyses of rationalization and bureaucracy in modern societies, and Arnold Schoenberg's abandonment of the musical organizing principle of tonality are paradigmatic for what concerns Adorno. The background to Adorno's work is also formed by the reception of Marx and Nietzsche, whose influence in Europe grew in the wake of the First World War. In all these cases ideas from the past concerning society and politics, subjectivity, art, religion, morality, and the natural world are put in doubt, leaving the question of what should replace them. The devastation of the First World War gives this question a particular urgency, the war having shown what pent-up destructive forces could be unwittingly unleashed by modern forms of production, exchange, and technology.

Adorno's importance does not depend on his immediate reactions to the political events of the Weimar Republic and beyond, but rather on his explorations of how these affect the arts, philosophy, and the social sciences. His earlier work consists mainly of his academic dissertations, other texts on phenomenology and existentialism which are increasingly influenced by the Marxist tradition, and writings on music and literature. It is the writings in American exile that appear in Europe after the war which begin to establish his reputation. His approach to the culture of his time is relentlessly critical, being famous for dicta like 'the whole is the untrue', 'to write poetry after Auschwitz is barbaric', 'there is no right way of living in life that is wrong', and for its stringency with respect to art which he thinks merely contributes to the status quo, rather than being aesthetically challenging. But what does he propose as an alternative to a world dominated by the destructive effects of modern capitalism? Any response to that question for Adorno depends on coming to terms with the Holocaust and the Nazi period, and the perversion of socialist ideas in communist countries. Without an understanding of what made such things possible, and the creation of a culture that would make a repetition impossible, hope for lasting human progress seems to him delusory.

In this context it should be remembered that in the years immediately following the war the Federal Republic of Germany did not engage in a thorough reckoning with the past. Many lawyers, doctors, scientists, and academics who had supported the Nazis remained in the same jobs, ex-Nazis played major political roles, and discussion of the Nazi period was often avoided in the name of rebuilding the devastated country as quickly as possible. Psychoanalyst Alexander Mitscherlich talked of 'the inability to mourn' as being characteristic of Germany at the time. Instead of facing up to what happened, in order to understand it and make changes, people's attention and energy were displaced into reconstruction of the country's infrastructure. Adorno, in contrast, played an influential role in keeping the issue of the Nazi past alive, beginning, while still in the USA, with *Dialectic of Enlightenment*, and with his participation in the Berkeley Anti-Semitism project. In 1959 he gave a lecture on 'What is coming to terms with the past?' in which he maintains that

'National Socialism lives on' (GS 10.2 p. 556) in various forms in German society. The lecture is notable for its complete repudiation of the tendency in Germany to repress critical discussion of the Nazi period.

It is no coincidence, then, that the substantial public reception of *Dialectic of Enlightenment* does not begin until the 1960s, when it is read by many in the Student Movement, and, having first been published in Holland, is finally published in Germany in 1969. The Student Movement was the result of a conviction among young Germans that the Federal Republic was becoming more authoritarian and undemocratic. Anger at this was focused by the killing in Berlin by the police of a protester against a visit of the Shah of Iran in 1967, and the shooting of Rudi Dutschke, a student activist, by a far-right extremist in 1968. Adorno's view of the way Nazism lived on, and his criticisms of the direction of modern societies resonated with the student protesters. The motivation of the protesters was fuelled by the failure of their parents' generation to confront the injustices of the past and their consequences in the present. The complexity of responding to the Nazi past is demonstrated by the fact that, with the ebbing of the Movement, some participants became terrorists in the Red Army Faction, while others moved into mainstream politics (these divergent responses are insightfully dealt with in Margarethe von Trotta's film, *Die bleierne Zeit*, released in English as *The German Sisters*). Although Adorno heavily criticized the more radical forms of action of the Movement, he encouraged the critical engagement with the status quo and entrenched conventions that was vital to the Movement (Figure 1). The hopes of a revolutionary change involving the working class on the part of the Movement were, as Adorno expected, soon dashed, but the lasting legacy of the period was that the Federal Republic, for all its faults, became a more open and democratic society.

It is characteristic of Adorno that, during the last period of his life, when political unrest was widespread and he was involved in very

1. **Adorno with leaders of the Student Movement.**

difficult institutional encounters with protesting students, he was also trying to write his major theoretical works on philosophy and aesthetics. His work tries to steer a course between attention to institutional, historical, and political factors, and their wider theoretical implications. It can lack the mass of empirical detail of the kind which Hannah Arendt, for example, offers in *The Origins of Totalitarianism*. Arendt herself does not, though, always convincingly explain the functioning of the relationships between the actions of individuals, and the varying social, cultural, and economic pressures that influence them, that are a major focus for Adorno. In an area as fraught as this no analysis is going to be definitive, and both Adorno's and Arendt's perspectives remain important as warnings against the recurrence of fascist politics.

Adorno's acute sense of the historical situatedness of thought, his suspicion of positive metaphysical claims, and his insistence on the importance of art can, as we will see, be used to question many dominant approaches to philosophy, and to illuminate pressing social and political issues. In *Aesthetic Theory* Adorno asserts that 'Already before Auschwitz it was an affirmative lie in the face of historical experiences to attribute any positive sense to existence. That has consequences right into the form of works of art' (GS 7 p. 229). He always insists that the appalling brutality of history must be kept in mind; at the same time, though, he is sensitive to the need to give expression to what is repressed and neglected in history, that may be a source of hope. The growing contemporary importance of Adorno's thought derives, then, from its attention to how to make sense in a world where so much militates against being able to do so.

Chapter 2
The modern subject

Enlightenment and dialectic

The title of *Dialectic of Enlightenment* (*DE*) (first published 1944)
highlights themes which are germane to all of Adorno's work.
'Enlightenment' is often characterized as the movement, starting
sometime in the 17th century, which uses reason to illuminate
what was previously obscured by myth, religion, and superstition.
'Dialectic', in the German traditions to which Adorno belongs,
refers to understanding how things turn into their opposites. The
concern is, then, with understanding change, rather than with
what, like the laws of nature, remains the same. As Adorno puts it,
in dialectical thinking 'everything is always only what it is by
becoming what it isn't' (GS 3 p. 32). The version of dialectic
proposed by G. W. F. Hegel (1770–1831) is one of the main
philosophical influences on Adorno. For Hegel, the fact that ideas
held as true—such as Ptolemy's earth-centred view of the
universe—come to be refuted is not a reason to espouse
scepticism, but rather the way in which we learn more truths
about the world. Copernicus needs Ptolemy to refute; otherwise
he has nothing to improve on. Hegel terms this refutation of a
specific existing claim that leads to a better one 'determinate
negation'. In dialectics things in opposition to each other also
belong together, because they depend on each other to be
manifest: you can't have the true without the false.

The chapter of *DE* on 'The Concept of Enlightenment' opens as follows: 'Enlightenment in the most all-encompassing sense of progressing thought has always pursued the goal of liberating people from fear and installing them as masters. But the completely enlightened earth radiates in the sign of triumphant calamity' (GS 3 p. 19). What aims at liberation 'dialectically' turns into its opposite, and the question is why this happens. The historical context of the end of the Second World War obviously made such questions very urgent. At issue here is the very status of 'reason'. Enlightenment reason makes it possible to gain technological mastery for human ends, but the effects of such mastery can be unreasonable, as the effects of technology on the war made clear. Reason can therefore in some sense be seen as contradictory. Unlike many philosophers, though, Adorno does not think that contradictions must necessarily be resolved, because contradiction for him is not just a logical issue, being instead inherent in our experience of the world. Consequently: 'the depth of a philosophy does not lie in the extent to which this philosophy can reconcile contradictions, but rather in the extent to which it is able to make contradictions manifest which are inherent in the matter itself'. So what contradictions are inherent in the notion of reason?

Reason and power

It might seem best in a philosophical discussion of 'reason' to give a definition of what is meant by the term before investigating it, but this is not Adorno's strategy. The problem is that a definition of 'reason' must presumably be 'rational', but the status of rationality itself is what is in question here: what would make the definition rational? There is no definitive way out of this dilemma, which touches on the very status of philosophy itself. On the assumption that there is no foundational certainty with respect to philosophical terms, one of Adorno's strategies is to see how those terms emerged and evolved historically. He is here influenced by Nietzsche's reflections on the way power relates to thinking:

reason as a way of mastering things: 'means–ends reason'—which Adorno refers to as 'instrumental reason'—is itself a form of power. His question is why this power leads to calamity in the form of totalitarianism, extermination camps, and technology-driven warfare.

The need to master things is obviously necessary to the survival of living beings, but mastery must also be seen from the side of what is mastered. Even the term 'mastery', with its masculine connotations, can involve a sense of repression of the other. If what is mastered is itself also a manifestation of power, the scenario becomes one of a conflict between warring powers, as it does in Nietzsche's idea of the 'Will to Power' as the essential basis of all existence. With respect to nature it can then seem that the human drive for survival must entail the defeat of an enemy through knowledge of its powers. Descartes famously talked of knowledge making us 'lords and owners of nature', and Francis Bacon maintained that knowledge of causal necessity in nature is the basis of human power: 'nor can nature be commanded except by being obeyed. And so those twin objects, human knowledge and human power, do really meet in one'. Adorno and Horkheimer suggest that the need for knowledge-based control can lead to the drive for omnipotence on the part of the subject, and this is precisely what can turn into its opposite: 'the more uninhibitedly reason...makes itself to the absolute opposite of nature...the more it regresses, as self-preservation run wild, to nature' (GS 6 p. 285). By regarding nature just as a threat to be controlled, or as a consumable resource, we end up threatening the survival of the civilized life we seek to preserve.

What is important here, and elsewhere in Adorno, is that the human subject is both part of nature and necessarily sets itself up against nature. He uses the psychoanalytical notion of 'projection', the displacing of one's own feelings, which are part of our nature that we cannot fully control, onto others, to analyse the relationship between humankind and nature. Projection occurs, for example, if you see the other person as angry when it is you that is angry, but can't acknowledge your negative feeling. In a section on the origin and persistence of anti-Semitism, *DE* extends this notion to include projection onto the world as a whole of the subject's states of mind, so taking the way humankind has come to treat the world as akin to the projections of the paranoid individual: 'In both cases the subject is in the centre, the world just the occasion of its delusion; the world becomes the impotent or omnipotent incarnation of what is projected onto it' (GS 3 p. 216).

Before the development of modern science, cultures employed mythology as a way of controlling nature in the imagination. Without some sense that mythology was in touch with nature, it would evidently not be effective for those who live in terms of it. The problem lies in knowing where imaginative projection stops and reality begins: in consequence, if there is 'insufficient differentiation by the subject of its own and the external share of the projected material', then 'In a certain sense all perception is projection' (GS 3 p. 213). The boundary between what is inside and what is outside cannot be clearly established, and the drive for mastery of fear is therefore likely to generate delusion. The usual idea is that modern science dispels such delusion, but this is precisely what Adorno and Horkheimer (Figure 2) want to investigate more carefully. Modern science produces true explanations, but it does so in contexts where the basis of mythology—the drive to master perceived threats—remains in place. These threats, of course, come to include new ones produced by science itself, and this situation is central to the notion of a 'dialectic of Enlightenment'.

Kant

For Adorno the very idea of an 'objective world' develops historically out of what is necessary for human survival. Throughout his career a key historical figure in focusing this issue

2. Horkheimer and Adorno.

is Immanuel Kant (1724–1804), whom he first read as a young man together with his friend, cultural theorist Siegfried Kracauer. *DE* cites Kant's 1781 *Critique of Pure Reason*, where the notion of 'schematism'—the 'hidden art in the depths of the human soul whose true workings we are unlikely ever to be able to divine from nature'—is used to explain how a shared objective, intelligible world can result from the mass of sensory input received by individual human subjects. Seeing both a bonsai and a giant redwood as trees involves the mind using a 'schema' which abstracts from their very evident differences to show what is identical about them. The reduction of difference to identity by the subject is crucial to Kant's theory of knowledge, and to Adorno's repeated explorations of Kant as an expression of the nature of the modern world: 'Without such schematism, in short, without the intellectuality of perception, no impression would fit a concept, no category an example, there would not even be unity of thought, let alone of the system that everything is aimed at' (GS 3 p. 102). The question is why something so necessary to exploring and understanding the world can also become a threat.

Adorno and Horkheimer's reading of Kant in *DE* is characteristically unorthodox: 'The true nature of schematism, which coordinates universal and particular, concept and individual instance, shows itself in contemporary science in the last analysis as the interest of industrial society' (GS 3 p. 103). This is because industry gains mastery over nature by reducing it to what can be manipulated in repeatable ways. *DE* turns Kant's epistemological argument into an anthropological account of the genesis of cognition: 'The system of things, the solid universe of which science only forms the abstract expression' becomes 'the unconsciously realised product of animal equipment in the fight for life' (GS 3 p. 213). This reading of Kant shows something vital about Adorno's relationship to philosophy. Kant is very often read as an epistemologist who wants to show how knowledge is possible via explanation of the ways the mind orders the information it receives from the world. He saw his philosophy as involving a 'Copernican turn' away from seeking the pre-existing truth of a divinely made objective world. Objectivity itself depends instead on the activity of the mind, which relates things to each other in specific, rule-bound ways. He does not, though, explain how and why the subject comes to function in this way. This is why *DE* attempts, in the light of its questions about the real nature of Enlightenment, to give a genetic account of subjectivity, in order to understand the dialectic it involves.

When writing about Kant and other philosophers, Adorno often does not primarily focus on the validity of their arguments, but looks instead at what the problems in an approach tell us about historical tensions of which they are a manifestation. Even if, for example, Kant's new account of the relationship between freedom and determinism is flawed, it can still be a vital resource in exploring why the modern world turns out the way it does. Adorno, then, wants to circumvent the tendency to see the history of philosophy as a history of error, which can lead to thinkers being written off, as Kant was for a time in the mid-20th century in the anglophone philosophical world. Kant's philosophy is, instead, a 'force-field', where 'behind the most abstract concepts which come into conflict with each other ... stand what are in reality extraordinarily vivid forces of experience'. The experience in question consists in humankind's attempts to understand itself and the world without relying on theology. As such: 'the power of the *Critique of Pure Reason* does not at all really lie so much in the answer which Kant gives to the so-called metaphysical questions, as it does in the very heroic, very stoical refusal to give an answer to these questions at all'. Adorno does not ignore what he calls the 'metaphysical need' to make sense of human existence, but neither does he think that philosophy has answers to it that have 'timeless truth valid for all future experience'.

Adorno's focus on Kant is based on the 'tension between the interest in the objectivity of truth, on the one hand, and the reflection on the knowing subject as that which constitutes such truth, on the other'. What does this tension reveal about the modern world, beyond Kant's own attempt to resolve it? Kant essentially transfers the idea of natural necessity from the side of the object to that of the subject, and this shift explains why Adorno sees the subject/object relationship in dialectical terms. Natural laws describe how, if x happens, y necessarily follows it. David Hume (1711–76) had pointed out, though, that all the evidence for such causal laws comes from subjects observing x and y being 'constantly conjoined'. The basis of the law therefore depended on the subject's perceptions, there being no justification for saying that the causal relationship was present in the things themselves. This made future events contingent, as they can only be inferred from what happened to have been observed in the past, with no guarantee that the same will be observed in the future. Any appeal to an inherent, God-given order in the universe could therefore not be justified in philosophy. The only order that there can be said to be is a result of human observation and judgement.

Kant accepts that Hume has shown that 'dogmatic' (i.e. theological) accounts of the order of things cannot be philosophically justified.

At the same time, it is clear that modern science, especially in the form of Newton's laws of motion, gives us a better account of the movement of bodies in nature than what preceded it. He therefore proposes to establish what it is that makes Newton's laws possible. The subject's observation of nature is necessary for this, which involves the object-side, because we don't control what perceptions we receive. However, he then argues that the necessity present in laws of nature must be produced by the subject linking perceptions together in rule-bound ways, otherwise, as we saw, there would just be a chaos of sensory input.

This much is standard fare in philosophical accounts of Kant. What Adorno focuses on, though, are the wider implications of the—dialectical—'turn' from ancient to modern epitomized by Kant, which locates objectivity in the subject's thinking, rather than seeing it as inherent in the world. This reversal plays out in myriad dimensions of modern history, and Kant is seen by Adorno as crystallizing this history in philosophical form. In this interpretation Adorno comes close to his contemporary Martin Heidegger's idea that modern philosophy begins with Descartes's grounding of philosophy in the putative certainty of the 'I think, I am', which means he sees the modern subject as that which seeks to dominate the object. Adorno's relationship to Heidegger, who was, of course, a member of the Nazi party, is too complex to be dealt with here, but their political differences, quite understandably, made Adorno underplay their philosophical proximity.

Adorno adds a psychoanalytical dimension to his account of the subject, as we saw, by suggesting that the subject's fear of the other, and its drive to control it, lead the subject to project onto the world. The combination of a Kantian and a psychoanalytical view of the subject means, on the one hand, that justified knowledge depends on the subject's forms of thinking, but, on the other, that these forms are linked to a drive to control nature that can become destructive. In consequence—and this suggests why the freedom/determinism issue is central in Kant—'what appears to us as autonomous, powerful subject keeps on revealing itself as conditioned, as dependent on what there is'. The subject seeks to establish a post-theological order of nature, but in doing so 'the mind which forgets its own origin in nature...more than ever falls prey to its origin in nature'. The human form of control over non-human nature leads to what Marx calls 'second nature', a human social world which can be just as threatening to the subject as the 'first' nature it seeks to control. Kant's philosophy therefore shows how the subject is both the source of cognitive and technological control of nature, and yet can be blind to how it is itself part of that nature.

Kant famously argues that we can only know how nature appears to us, not how it is 'in itself', thus establishing what Adorno calls the Kantian 'block' between the subject and being. Adorno says that the *Critique of Pure Reason* 'is at the same time a philosophy of identity—i.e. a philosophy which attempts finally to ground being in the subject and a philosophy of non-identity, insofar as it tries to limit this claim to identity...through the *block* that the subject encounters in its cognition'. Adorno's notion of 'non-identity' suggests that the ways in which the world is ordered, such as by the commodity form, can always hide other ways in which it can be responded to. The modern growth of knowledge brings untold benefits, but also the following: 'The more the world is emptied of an objective meaning [of the kind he suggests is present in Plato and pre-modern theology and philosophy] and is completely resolved into our categories, so completely becomes *our* world, the more meaning is removed from the world at the same time'. 'Meaning' here is not primarily linguistic, but has to do with what makes sense of the world. The world created by modern rationality and modern forms of exchange, for all the benefits it brings, does not always become more hospitable to humankind. What societies actually invest in knowing is influenced to a significant extent by the drive to exercise power, as the amounts spent on military research and the production of arms suggest.

Hegel

Adorno contrasts Kant's refusal to give cognition wholesale command over how we relate to the world with aspects of the 'philosophy of identity' he sees in German Idealism, and in Hegel in particular. Understanding Adorno depends to a great extent, along with understanding Kant, on grasping certain key ideas in German Idealism. German Idealism is a reaction from the 1790s onwards to the perception that Kant had created a gap between humankind and the true nature of the world. The gap was seen as threatening to lead to scepticism—if we do not know the world as it is in itself, how can we say we know the truth about the world? It was also, though, thought of as a form of 'alienation' from nature, whose real essence was hidden from us, and needed to be either uncovered or recovered. One route to overcoming the perceived split is seen as developing a philosophy which systematically articulates how subject and object relate, without leaving the residue of the 'thing in itself'. Hegel argues that the 'thing in itself' is actually a product of thinking: it is what results when we subtract everything we know of an object from the object. This leaves us with an empty abstraction, as opposed to the diverse cognitive and other experience we actually have of a real object in the world. Thought is, as such, inherently 'of the world', in the sense that it belongs to the world as something which changes and develops, and the point is to explicate how this is the case. In one respect Adorno agrees, and he echoes Hegel's argument: 'the supposedly pure object that is free of the addition of thought and perception is precisely the reflex of abstract subjectivity' (GS 10.2 p. 748). The dialectical thinking Adorno espouses rejects a radical split between subject and object, but he differs from Hegel on how their relationship can be articulated in philosophy.

Hegel both proposes an all-encompassing philosophical system and shows how contradiction is inseparable from thinking. Adorno adopts the latter idea, but questions the idea that these two sides of Hegel are fully compatible. In seeking to construct a philosophical system, modern philosophy is faced with the problem of how to establish a foundation for it. The traditional response to this is theological: the founding principle upon which everything rests is God, so the aim is to explicate the intelligibility of nature imbued in it by the creator. In Spinoza's pantheism, which heavily influenced German Idealism, God actually is Nature, qua the totality of the universe. Spinoza talks of 'God or Nature', and maintains that there is no split between mind and nature: 'the mind understands itself the better, the more it understands of Nature'. Hegel develops a version of this idea in the *Phenomenology of Spirit* (1807): rather than being the eternal, unchanging principle of which everything that exists is a manifestation, the substance of the universe is active and develops to higher stages, as the 'becoming of itself'. It does so for Hegel precisely because it involves contradiction: it opposes itself to itself by moving from opaque unity to being the developed multiplicity of an intelligible world.

In Hegel's terms, if we think of the notion of the universe, in the sense of 'everything there is', as 'being', we have thought 'nothing', because there is no content to the notion: saying 'everything is' is hardly very informative. The contradiction that emerges from the idea of 'being' forces us to try and give content to the idea by specifying *what* things are. The system which is to explicate the nature of things is a dynamic system of 'negations': things gain their identity by being opposed to other things—red is not blue, etc.—and the very notion of colour changes, as it becomes what it previously was not, when science and art reveal more about it. In Hegel's terms the 'essence' of something is not, therefore, its timeless true nature, but rather its dynamic development, which he exemplifies by the development of a seed into a plant. The truth of philosophy is a progressing illumination of things by overcoming what is lacking in each particular manifestation of thought, and the final truth is the systematically articulated whole of the development. Each part of this is temporal and dependent on other parts; the whole, though, transcends time and does not depend on anything else. In sum, as Hegel says: 'the whole is the true'.

When Adorno says that 'the whole is the untrue', he is, then, directly opposed to Hegel, but they still concur in certain respects. Both think that things can only be understood by their links to the whole in which they are located, which involves development through contradiction. The question that separates them, therefore, is how one conceives of the 'whole'. Hegel's core idea is that what he calls 'immediacy', where something is not related to anything else—like the notion of 'being'—cannot be the basis of thought, and Adorno also uses versions of this idea in many contexts. Hegel also opposes the idea of a philosophy based on an initial, immediate foundation, such as Descartes's foundation of certainty in the 'I think, I am'. Instead of being fully given at the outset, the I is what develops as the subject matures via its interactions with the world. Adorno concurs that 'first philosophy', like that of Descartes or Husserl, cannot be defended: 'there is no such last thing, nothing absolutely given and purified of all mediations, be it Husserlian pure consciousness or empiricist pure sensuous datum'. Both he and Hegel refuse, then, to see consciousness and the world as separate, because each 'mediates' the other, changing what the other actually is.

Where Adorno and Hegel radically differ is in the way they interpret the relationship between universal and particular. Hegel sees universal ways of grasping the world that develop through mediation as culminating in philosophy systematically explaining the nature of mind/spirit [*Geist*] as, in some still disputed sense, the world making *itself* intelligible. The overarching whole is constituted by the 'subject' side, which leads Hegel to use terms like 'world-spirit' to characterize the collective result of mind's historical development. Institutions and structures, such as legal systems, become effective despite the often conflicting and confused intentions of the individuals who constitute them: Hegel refers to this as the 'cunning of reason'. Philosophy's job is to reveal the rationality in the confusions of the everyday world, so that we come to understand ourselves better, and are willing to accept the necessity of restrictions imposed by forms like the law.

Adorno thinks Hegel underestimates the dangers in how these societal structures determine those located within them. Far from always being rational manifestations of '*Geist*', the structures can be the result of objective pressures that subjugate people, such as those produced by the capitalist market of commodity exchange. In this 'individuals are relegated to being mere organs for the implementation of the universal' (GS 6 p. 336). As he bluntly puts it: 'the impotence of spirit [*Geist*] in relation to reality was demonstrated in a probably unparalleled manner' by the events of the Hitler era. Consequently: 'The reasonableness of history can only prove itself in terms of *for whom* history really is reasonable'. In a society riven by class and racial oppression, the philosophical command Hegel seeks as part of a story of progressing rationality, becomes, for Adorno, an ideology of the status quo.

'Nature-history'

Marx and other 'Young Hegelians' had already made objections like this to Hegel, but Adorno does so in the wake of the Holocaust, which puts philosophical attempts to see rationality in history even more drastically in question. For Adorno the law is 'the primal phenomenon of irrational rationality. In it the formal principle of equivalence becomes the norm, the hiding place of the inequality of the equal, in which differences are obliterated' (GS 6 pp. 303–4). He is not against the principle of equality before the law, but the historical reality is that the law often leads to injustice: 'legal norms cut off what is not covered by them, every experience of the specific, for the sake of seamless classification'

(GS 6 p. 304). Poet, journalist, and novelist, Anatole France's (1844–1924) comment that 'In its majestic equality, the law forbids rich and poor alike to sleep under bridges, beg in the streets and steal loaves of bread' suggests the problem. As does the fact that the establishment of the American Constitution, claiming 'All men are created equal', was in part the work of slave-owners. Hegel maintains that the development of the universality of law is what enables us to have rights and recourse to justice at all, by reconciling conflicting interests and demands. Adorno sees such universal forms as being capable of producing the opposite of what was intended, as the bureaucratic and legal sides of Nazism showed. He cites Hegel: 'As the state, the fatherland constitutes a commonality of existence, as the subjective will of people subordinates itself to the law, the opposition between freedom and necessity disappears' (in GS 6 p. 344). In the light of history after Hegel, where modern states can degenerate into agents of mass oppression, Adorno regards this attempt to overcome the split between freedom and necessity as fundamentally misguided, though he tends, as his pupil Jürgen Habermas suggests, to underestimate how the law can sometimes also function as a crucial bastion against oppression.

Once again, then, as he did in relation to Kant, Adorno points to how the forms of identification and classification generated by the modern subject to control nature can become objective forces which damage subjects. The dual sense of 'subject' here is central to Adorno's dialectical approach: 'subject can refer to the single individual as well as to universal determinations, in the language of Kant's *Prolegomena*, to "consciousness in general". The equivocation cannot simply be removed by terminological clarification. For both meanings reciprocally require each other; the one is hardly to be understood without the other' (GS 10.2 p. 741). The subject is in one sense that which seeks to overcome nature, as the object which threatens it, but 'Human history, the history of progressing command of nature, carries on the consciousness-less history of nature, eat and be eaten' (GS 6 pp. 348–9). The consequence of the command sought by the collective human subject is that individual, embodied, vulnerable subjects can be at the mercy of the collective product of their *own* actions. Adorno here follows Marx, citing this passage from Marx's *Grundrisse* (1857–61) on the 'nature-history' of humankind:

> Just as much as the whole of this movement appears as a social process, and just as much as the individual moments of this movement begin with the conscious will and particular aims of individuals, just as much does the totality of the process appear as an objective context, which arises naturally; it admittedly results from the interaction of conscious individuals, but is neither located in their consciousness, nor is subsumed as a whole under them. (cit. GS 6 p. 349)

Hegel, Marx, and Adorno, then, all see subject and object as always already affecting each other in such a way that the very terms 'subjective' and 'objective' do not have fixed meanings, and have to be understood through their historical contexts: 'Objectivity is only recognisable by reflecting at every historical stage and every stage of cognition on that which presents itself in each case as subject and as object, and on their mediations' (GS 10.2 p. 752). 'Subjective' consciousness is therefore not something internal to the individual, because its content is substantially determined by objective social and economic influences.

This leads Adorno to a further way of interpreting Kant's notion of the 'transcendental subject', the condition of possibility of objectivity, in terms of political economy: 'In the doctrine of the transcendental subject the precedence is manifest of the abstract rational relations that have been separated from individual people and their relationships, that have their model in exchange' (GS 10.2 p. 745). In answer to the question of how to think of the split between the transcendental subject and the particular empirical, embodied subject, Adorno therefore suggests: 'The living single person, as they are forced to act...is, as embodied homo oeconomicus, more the transcendental subject than the living single person as which they must immediately take themselves' (GS 10.2 p. 745). Whereas Hegel sees the totality of social relations as generating rational insight, Adorno sees it in terms of social and economic forms produced by the subject which can become objective hindrances to individual human flourishing. He therefore argues that the relationship between 'history', as the location of human action, and 'nature', as the unchanging context of that action, has to be rethought. We will look at some consequences of this in the next chapter.

Chapter 3
Nature and history

The dialectic of culture

Adorno rejects the assumption, as he does in relation to other terms, that 'nature' and 'history' have to be given definitions:

> You know that I am not at all fond of definitions. Perhaps I could add that the concept of definition has been most emphatically criticised in great philosophy, one after the other by Kant, by Hegel, finally also by Nietzsche, but that this criticism has been afflicted with the curse of impotence.

The content of terms emerges rather from seeking to understand their interaction: this may well involve attempts at definition, but the definitions will be provisional. As such, in modern history, the situation arises where 'historical conditions...present themselves as natural conditions' (GS 6 p. 352), but, at the same time, what seem to be natural conditions are actually historical, because how we understand nature depends on human history. This apparent paradox is central to Adorno's thinking, but evidently needs some explanation. As we saw, 'second nature'—human society—threatens humankind just as 'first nature' does, and also, in turn, changes how 'first nature' is understood. This reversal is part of Adorno's wider questioning of metaphysics, which is summed up by his contention: 'That the unchanging is truth, and the mobile, transient mere appearance, the indifference of temporal and eternal ideas to each other, can no longer be asserted' (GS 6 p. 354). The modern world involves what Max Weber terms 'disenchantment', which ensues from the successes of modern science: 'one can, in principle, master all things by calculation. This means that the world is disenchanted' ('Science as Vocation'). Instead of the essentially theological idea that meaning is objectively imbued in things, meaning now becomes something which is continually in question, and gains a fundamentally historical aspect. The new insights of physics also give rise to existential questions which do not have scientific answers. If the objective truth about the physical universe arrived at by calculation is that it will, according to the law of entropy, 'die' in the 'heat death of the universe', does anything in life actually matter at all, because it all comes to an end anyway? At the same time, the finitude and transience of the physical universe in the form we know it need not lead to meaninglessness. The opposite can be the case: if the only place there is meaning is in our finite existence, finite things can matter more, rather than less, because there is nowhere else for things to matter. The question is now *how* they matter, and that is a central concern for Adorno.

While acknowledging the importance of transitory meanings, Adorno contends that the fact that Auschwitz was possible means any attempt to give universal meaning to human existence has to confront humankind's capacity for the complete destruction of meaning: 'That it could happen in the midst of all the tradition of philosophy, of art and enlightening sciences says more than only that *Geist* ("mind/spirit") was unable to take hold of people and change them' (GS 6 p. 359). What makes Auschwitz possible is therefore inherent in that tradition itself. This is the core of Adorno's critical conception of modernity, and it involves a further contradiction. In 'On the Concept of History', written in 1940 (not long before his suicide in France when he thought his attempt to escape the Nazis had failed), Walter Benjamin had said of cultural treasures:

They owe their existence not only to the efforts of the great minds and talents who have created them, but also to the anonymous toil of their contemporaries. There is no document of civilization which is not at the same time a document of barbarism. And just as such a document is not free of barbarism, barbarism taints also the manner in which it was transmitted from one owner to another.

It is not that culture therefore has no value: Adorno also characteristically insists that 'whoever refuses culture directly promotes the barbarism as which culture has revealed itself' (GS 6 p. 360). At the same time culture's complicity in the history in which it is located cannot be ignored. The dialectic here illustrates why Adorno proposes what he calls 'negative dialectics'. Culture also becomes its opposite (barbarism), but this does not mean that philosophy, as part of that culture, gains higher insight: rather 'thought, in order to be true, would have, today at least, also to think against itself' (GS 6 p. 358). In this situation there is no guarantee that thought will not continue to promote barbarism: thinking demands continual critical 'self-reflection', with no certainty that it is not contributing to delusion.

The consequence is that the apparently best justified ways of thinking may turn out to be unsustainable. In negative dialectics, unlike in Hegel's dialectic, what results from a contradiction need not generate greater insight. It is, therefore, not enough for philosophers to assume they are seeking the truth: they should also reflect on how what they are doing affects the contexts in which they do this: 'There is no construct in the world, not the highest constructs of philosophy, not the highest of art, which could not, by holding onto them in an isolated manner, be misused to keep people away from other things, to deceive people about other matters'. The focus of much modern philosophy is on the sciences and on the justification of scientific knowledge, but this has arguably led philosophy to underplay interpretation of the effects of the sciences in real-world circumstances. Locating the natural sciences' search for an objective account of nature in wider contexts leads Adorno to his interrogation of the relationship between 'nature' and 'history'.

Nature

'Nature' in one sense is just 'everything', from the material of the universe to the ways it becomes organized, including whatever consciousness is seen to be, on the assumption that without its natural conditions of possibility there would be no consciousness. But the idea of 'nature' needs an 'other' to contrast with, if it is to have any determinate content. The metaphysical idea that 'the unchanging is truth' can apply to some conceptions of 'nature', of the kind which underpin the modern natural sciences. These investigate nature as a system of unchanging laws, as opposed to the changing world of history. Kant speaks in this respect of the 'formal' sense of nature as a 'totality of rules', and as 'the lawfulness of appearances in space and time'. This raises the question of how we, as parts of physical nature, can be free and not just determined by that nature, and this makes us the 'other' to nature in some sense.

Kant argued that natural necessity actually depends on the ways we think: the 'highest legislation of nature must lie in ourselves'. If human existence plays out in history, this already suggests that a strict division between nature as the realm of unchanging laws, and history as the realm of human action, can be questioned. The sense of 'nature' thus becomes something contested. This is not just a theoretical issue, because assumptions about the division between nature and culture—for example in relation to judgements on how responsible people are for their actions, or questions of sex and gender—have major consequences in many areas of human life, from the law, to psychology, to education.

One of Adorno's pupils, philosopher Albrecht Wellmer, suggests that a very different sense of nature is also involved in Adorno:

Theodor W. Adorno

'The nature which we, as acting and deliberating creatures, are aware of as our own nature—the nature Adorno speaks of—is not the nature of scientifically objectified brain processes, but the living nature of our body with its neediness, its impulses, its potentials and its vulnerability'. These are not fully under our control, because they also depend on our biology, and culture both inhibits and enables expressions of our impulses. This nature is inevitably changed by the contexts which people inhabit, and so is also historical. The approach here is at odds with the kind of 'naturalist' theory which seeks to explain human action in terms of law-bound internal mechanisms, of the kind used to explain non-human nature. Even the status of non-human nature is, though, not something unchanging: it moves historically, for example, from being God's creation to being the contested modern concept we are considering here. The emergence of landscape painting in the West from the Renaissance onwards, where the human figure ceases to be the main focus, suggests another dimension of nature's history. In a more troubling sense, intrusions into domains previously untouched by humankind, which, for example, can unleash new viruses like HIV or Covid-19, also point to a historical dimension of 'nature'.

Adorno maintains that the 'question of nature as something absolutely primary, as absolutely immediate in relation to its mediations', is 'deceptive' (GS 6 p. 353). He cites Marx and Engels (Figure 3): 'history can be considered from two sides, be divided into the history of nature and the history of humankind. But the two sides cannot be separated; as long as people exist the history of nature and the history of people condition each other' (cited in GS 6 p. 351). This leads to another dialectical reversal, which sees 'everything historical as nature, precisely because it still remains...under the spell of the blind context of the nature which it pushes away from itself'. The 'spell of the blind context of nature' exerts itself in the ways that social humankind opposes the threats of external nature, but thereby produces equivalent threats in society.

3. Marx and Engels.

Adorno illustrates seeing the 'historical as nature' by the example of nationalism, itself a historical phenomenon that develops at the end of the 18th century, but one which relies on supposedly natural factors, like ethnicity: 'Precisely because the nation is not nature, it must continually announce to itself that it really is something like proximity to nature, immediacy, community of the people'. The effects of this particular version of seeing history as nature remain, despite the experience of the Holocaust, one of the major determining factors in world politics, and Adorno regarded it as a major task to reveal the deception it involves.

Second nature

For Adorno things which are taken as 'given' have historical and social aspects, and so could always have developed in other ways. The way things are at a particular time is neither predetermined nor a product of necessity: 'What we encounter as nature is in truth second nature and not first, and…we, in order to give abused and oppressed nature its due, must not allow ourselves to be blinded precisely by that appearance of the natural'. There is, as such, no access to what is 'essentially natural' or 'essentially historical', because seeking to establish a firm boundary between the two leads to ideological distortions. What the terms mean changes with history, and we cannot wholly transcend our own historical nature and gain a neutral 'view from nowhere'. We can, though, become aware of what we have previously abused and repressed because we only saw it as 'just the way things are': the ongoing battle against racism illustrates what is at issue here.

Thought itself is often seen as what separates us from nature, but once again this is not as simple as it might seem. Basing itself on an objectifying assumption about what nature essentially is, of the kind Adorno rejects, reductionist neuroscience tries to show that thought should be incorporated into nature seen as a system of laws, which leads to ideas like the brain as a computer and questions about 'artificial intelligence'. From Adorno's perspective, in contrast, thought functions as objective nature when it becomes what can increase rather than alleviate human distress or blocks possibilities of social improvement. Some (but by no means all) versions of neuroscience have the potential to do this, precisely by trying to reduce what Wellmer terms our 'living nature' to being a technocratically manipulable, objective process. Adorno's view of the thought/nature issue is illustrated when he discusses computers: 'They show to people the vacuity of formalised thinking that has been divested of its content, insofar as they are better able to carry out what the method of subjective reason i.e. the method of the natural sciences is proud of than are thinking subjects' (GS 10.2 p. 600). It is not, therefore, that computers have no value, but

> Philosophical thinking only begins as soon as it is not satisfied with knowledge that is expected and in which nothing more shows itself than one already put into it. The humane sense of computers would be to relieve the thought of living people to such an extent that it

would gain the freedom for knowledge that was not already implicitly present. (GS 10.2 p. 600)

Economist John Maynard Keynes had predicted in the 1930s that technology would replace most forms of work. The fact is that it hasn't, and very many people end up doing what anthropologist David Graeber has called 'bullshit jobs', in which 'technology has been marshalled, if anything, to figure out ways to make us all work more'. This suggests, in another example of a dialectic of Enlightenment, how the knowledge Adorno is concerned with, which would make society more fit for human beings, has too often failed to materialize, even as technological command has massively expanded.

So how should 'nature' be thought about? In lectures on *Problems of Moral Philosophy* Adorno makes a further dialectical claim: 'We are really no longer ourselves a piece of nature at the moment when we notice, when we recognize, that we are a piece of nature.' Instead of raising ourselves to the status of 'lord and owner' of nature, which objectifies it as 'the other', the realization that we are part of nature opens up the possibility of understanding how we might inhabit nature in ways that do less damage to it. Adorno refers to this as 'remembrance of nature in the subject' (GS 3 p. 58), and such understanding can also reduce the damage we do to ourselves. As with Adorno's conception of the subject, this leads to a dialectical contradiction. 'Nature' can be that which—following the German word for 'object', '*Gegenstand*'—'stands against' the subject and has in some measure to be resisted: this can include society when it becomes oppressive 'second nature'. 'Nature' can, however, also be what is oppressed by instrumental reason, to which philosophy, and art, should give a voice, thus seeing nature as 'subject', because it can suffer oppression. These senses of nature are clearly opposed to each other. There is, for Adorno, though, no way of definitively resolving such contradictions. The aim is to use them to sustain awareness of how our relationships to the world produce blindness to what they exclude—which is why thought needs to 'think against itself'. What is at issue here is apparent, for example, in the changed sense that 'nature' has taken on since the climate crisis and the threat of civilizational collapse have become ever more pressing concerns.

Mimesis

In order to explain the kinds of relationship to the world at issue here, Adorno introduces the idea of what he terms 'mimesis'. Following Aristotle, mimesis is often used to refer to conceptions of art that see it as 'representation' of reality (e.g. in a painting or a play), but it can also refer to forms of animal and human mimicry, and this is the aspect that initially concerns Adorno. He wants to characterize non-objectifying relationships to the world which are prior to conceptual thought: 'premundane mimesis, reflex-based imitation, the however vain stirring from which once emerged what is different from what is given: mind [*Geist*] itself' (GS 16 p. 227). Two examples he gives from the arts can help illustrate what he means. In a discussion of march elements in the music of Gustav Mahler, he suggests that marches 'always also dictate something to the people marching by mimetically pre-empting their step' (GS 13 p. 274). This happens at a level where people marching don't think about what they are doing, thus in a 'pre-reflexive' manner. The concert hall designed by architect Hans Scharoun for the Berlin Philharmonic Orchestra suggests how mimesis is not necessarily based on identity or similarity with things in the world, in the manner of a picture: 'in order to produce spatially ideal conditions for orchestral music' the hall 'becomes similar to music without borrowing from it' (GS 7 p. 73). The origins of mimesis are described thus: 'Magic, like science, pursues objectives, but it does so by mimesis, not in progressing distance from the object' (GS 3 p. 28). In science this distance results from applying universal concepts to differing particulars.

Mimesis involves a specific response to a specific object that does not seek to make it the same as other objects. Adorno infers a central point about language from this: 'But language, by virtue of its signifying element, the antithesis of the mimetic-expressive element, is chained to the form of judgement and proposition, and thence to the synthetic function of the concept' (GS 11 p. 471). This has significant consequences for his view of aesthetics: music precisely avoids the 'form of the judgement'—Adorno refers to 'judgementless synthesis' as crucial to art—and poetry has to find ways of dealing with the contradiction between the ways in which words signify by applying a universal to particulars, and the drive to express something that is not just the reduction of it to general terms (see Chapter 6). Mimesis is, then, an 'attitude to reality this side of the fixed opposition of subject and object', and without it 'the split of subject and object would be absolute and cognition impossible' (GS 7 p. 169). He talks of the 'mimetic moment of knowledge' as 'the elective affinity of knower and known' (GS 6 p. 55). One can see this in children's immediate sympathetic engagement with other living beings and things in the world, which does not rely on identification, and makes the development of cognitive engagement possible: 'If this moment were completely eradicated, the possibility of subject knowing object would be absolutely incomprehensible' (GS 6 p. 55), because there would be nothing initially motivating and directing it. The mimetic can blend with rationality, and this, Adorno contends, becomes apparent in '*Differenziertheit*', 'differentiatedness/complexity', thus in the ability to respond to unexpected detail that is missed or repressed by established ways of thinking. The mimetic belongs in one sense, therefore, on the side of 'nature', because it is not something learned via social rules. The mimetic is also vital to particular responses to things that are not to be reduced to the universal, which means it is also essential to 'history'.

The contemporary importance of these rather complex ideas lies in the way they offer a counter to the tendency to regard the natural sciences as the ultimate arbiter in our self-understanding. Wellmer makes the implication of Adorno's ideas clear, when he says:

It seems that we cannot reconstruct the history of nature, part of which is the emergence of human forms of life and of the spheres of subjective and objective spirit, in terms of a nomological [=based on laws] physical theory, precisely because to describe what is essentially *new* in the process of evolution we need categories beyond those of physics and not reducible to them.

The 'new' is normally associated with history, in opposition to nature as the ever-same, but the point Adorno and Wellmer make is that we need to be alert to how history and nature are dialectically related, and this precludes nature being 'the history-less, Platonically ontological' (GS 1 p. 349). Nothing that Adorno proposes here is intended to put in question the results of methodologically sound research in the physical sciences. However, philosophy needs to take account of the meaning and effects of the sciences in concrete human circumstances, which cannot be grasped in those sciences' own terms, and yet are part of the history of the nature which the sciences investigate. History in Hegel is the realm of self-determination, of 'freedom' in the sense derived from Kant, who saw it as the rational adherence to norms governing one's actions. In Adorno's view this conception fails to account for why history so often functions as 'nature', precisely by undermining self-determination. In consequence, he asks how 'freedom' can better be understood, and this will be the focus of the next chapter.

Chapter 4
History and freedom

Freedom as an empirical issue

Modern philosophical thinking about freedom often involves asking whether freedom exists at all. If everything that can be observed in the physical world functions in terms of deterministic laws, as modern science largely assumes it does, why should the physical object 'human being' be any different? What we regard as our freedom, which is the basis of our decisions on our actions, is in these terms located in the same chains of causality as everything else that happens, even though it may not seem that way to us. In the everyday world, in contrast, freedom is associated with the ability to do what one wants, unhindered by other individuals or by the state. That such freedom has to involve limits is generally accepted, but the nature of those limits is often ferociously contested. In philosophical accounts of these issues, a contrast is sometimes made between 'negative freedom', the absence of limits and constraints from outside oneself, and 'positive freedom', the capacity to act and exercise one's free will in a rational manner. The latter, of course, depends on being in a society which does not constrain my capacity to decide for myself. In a related vein, a distinction is made between questions of 'political freedom', which involve the constraints a society may legitimately impose on its members, and the metaphysical question we opened with, of 'freedom of the will', and whether it really exists. Adorno's responses to the issue of freedom are interesting not least because they question whether the directions just outlined really grasp the significance of 'freedom' in the modern world. His focus on the Holocaust can suggest why this might be the case. Are we to understand the way in which the perpetrators enacted unimaginable cruelty on such a scale in terms of people exercising their free will?

For Adorno freedom 'is a category which is *historical* through and through…one cannot, for example, formulate and stipulate a concept of freedom once and for all, in the way philosophy has almost always done it'. What is often seen as a metaphysical issue is, then, actually something empirical, that we all experience at various times: 'The contradiction between freedom and determinism is…one of the self-experience of subjects, sometimes free, sometimes unfree' (GS 6 p. 294). This might seem just to be referring to 'political freedom', but this is not the case, though he thinks the aim of such freedom is vital. Adorno does not focus on the metaphysical question of free will, precisely because it can exclude consideration of the fact that freedom and history are inseparable. There are good philosophical reasons for his approach. The very notion of a society that is more than just an aggregate of human beings requires the notion of freedom: 'Without any conception of freedom organised society could hardly be theoretically justified' (GS 6 p. 217). If one denies the existence of freedom, the following problem arises: 'In the situation of a complete determinism with no gaps, criteria of good and evil would be just completely meaningless, you couldn't even ask about them'. In seeking to reduce freedom to something else you have to invoke something that gives content to the term—how do we have any comprehension of *what* it is that doesn't exist? Telling protesters against a repressive government that what they seek doesn't really exist, because everything is determined, makes no sense. Even in the case of political freedom the question remains as to why such freedom matters at all, and this, as Adorno says, is a result of people's experience of freedom and unfreedom.

The idea that what appears to us to be freedom can really be explained by the correct physicalist account of the functioning of nature simply omits what is at issue, namely the roles freedom plays in human experience and action. Freedom is, then, dialectically constituted:

> Freedom becomes concrete in the changing forms of repression: in the resistance to these. There is as much freedom of the will as people wished to liberate themselves. Freedom itself is so tied up with unfreedom that it is not only inhibited by it, but has it as a condition of its own concept. (GS 6 p. 262)

The changing forms of this relationship can only be understood by looking at history, not by advancing a metaphysical argument for freedom of the will. Such an argument would be merely abstract, because it cannot encompass differing historical experiences of repression, and the specific forms taken by resistance to the repression.

Freedom and human practice

Freedom is, of course, also a precarious notion, because thinking or feeling that you are free can involve the danger of self-deception. This raises the question of how it is possible to know if you really are 'free'. For Adorno, taking account of the possibility of self-deception is vital to thinking about how ideology affects modern politics. Kant sees human behaviour as linked to our natural impulses, and so as largely determined by something other than freedom: we don't choose to have impulses or which impulses we have. Thinking you are free, because you are doing what you want, can therefore, as Rousseau argued, actually mean you are slave to your passions. Kant goes so far as to argue that we can never know if what we do is autonomous, because even doing good can be based on our action making us feel better, so is not done solely in terms of obeying a moral imperative. In order to bolster his notion of freedom he talks of a 'causality through freedom' that is required to set a new causal chain in motion, and which does not depend on a prior causal chain, of the kind that underlies our natural impulses and the laws of non-human nature.

Adorno, however, argues that we would only be free in Kant's sense if we did not fulfil our causally based 'natural' inclinations, and that Kant therefore requires the complete absence of 'nature' in our moral actions:

> If one just insisted on saying: there is admittedly something like freedom in the absolute, but as soon as I move into the limited realm of experience…there is only causality and you can't find any freedom, then nothing at all would be done for practice itself with this announcement of this principle of freedom. For practice is always the practice of empirical human beings which relates to empirically given circumstances.

As such: 'this double difficulty, that something like the sphere of the human can exist neither in absolute lawfulness nor in absolute freedom is really the most profound reason for Kant being forced into the paradoxical construction of a causality through freedom'. Reducing 'nature' to the realm of what is subject to necessary laws is, as we have seen, precisely what Adorno seeks to question. At the same time, 'freedom can only become real by going through the compulsion of civilisation, not as a retour à la nature' (GS 6 p. 151).

Adorno reads Kant's account of freedom in the manner we have seen him read other aspects of Kant, namely as a symptom of a real contradiction in modern life. Causal explanation functions in this perspective primarily as a means to control nature, including our own nature, in the form of technological 'instrumental reason'. How is this to be reconciled with the Enlightenment idea that freedom is the basis of meaningful human life? Kant's idea of freedom as self-determination by adherence to social duty can appear as a form of repression, in the psychoanalytical sense. Freedom is here another means of controlling nature—our nature—and arguably can make us *less* free: 'However, what happens in the most recent times is the externalisation of the superego into unconditional conformism, not its incorporation in a more rational whole' (GS 6 p. 271). A life spent denying the satisfactions of sensuous existence by wholesale subordination of oneself to duty is at odds with the experience of freedom as the overcoming of neurosis-inducing inhibitions which can be a source of cruelty to others. The 'truth content of neuroses is that they demonstrate to the I in itself, by what is alien to the I, by the feeling of "That isn't me at all", its unfreedom; there, where its command over inner nature fails' (GS 6 p. 222). Neuroses are 'Pillars of society; they thwart people's better potential, and with it the objectively better things that people could bring about' (GS 6 p. 293).

Kantian morality therefore leads to the following contradiction:

> In a certain sense the two contradictory moments of Kantian moral philosophy, namely the idea of freedom and the idea of, one has to say, suppression, above all of the suppression of any natural impulse—the suppression of inclination, the suppression of sympathy—both really only come about for the sake of freedom.

The pursuit of happiness is vital, for Adorno, to how we conceive of human freedom, and it seems 'incompatible with reason as a universal principle' in Kant. As such, the very point of reason itself becomes open to doubt, because Kant fails to answer the question 'whether the absolute realisation of reason would not mean something like the fulfilment of precisely everything that is suppressed by him' because it is part of the determined world of nature. This points to what Adorno sees as the Enlightenment's 'confusion of freedom with the business of self-preservation' (GS 3 p. 58), in the name of which socially repressive norms develop. In the same way as he questions the rigid opposition of history and nature, he questions Kant's separation of the causally determined world of appearance and the 'intelligible' realm of freedom in which action is not subject to natural causality.

The echoes of theological debates about the cause of the universe are informative here: if everything in the world has a cause, what caused the universe, and what stops a regress of causes of causes of the universe? The answer was often seen as God as the 'first cause', and this is echoed in the absolute, non-empirical status of Kant's notion of the subject's 'causality through freedom', as opposed to the relative status of all causes in the empirical world. So what is Adorno's alternative?

The history of freedom

Adorno questions the idea that the subject's either having or not having a capacity for 'absolute beginnings' is the key to freedom. Why should freedom be reducible to having a kind of on–off switch for doing x or not doing x that is not part of a causal chain, and has nothing to do with specific empirical circumstances? Kant's attempt to separate the empirical individual from the transcendental subject comes up against a problem in any case of a decision:

> the empirical subject that makes those decisions—and only an empirical subject can make them, the transcendental pure I think would not be capable of having impulses—is itself a moment of the spatio-temporal 'external' world and has no ontological priority to it; this is why the attempt to locate the question of freedom in it fails. (GS 6 p. 213)

Adorno often refers when considering such questions to the 'primacy of the objective' with respect to understanding the life of human subjects:

> For it is on the sphere of the objective, on the organisation of the world and the state of the world that the extent to which the subject attains autonomy depends.... Detached from the state of the world, autonomy is fictitious—or such a thin and abstract principle that nothing at all more can be said with it about the real and actual behaviour of people.

Sartre's insistence that even someone in a situation with no freedom to act at all remains somehow 'free', because they have a choice over how they relate to their situation, makes little sense to Adorno: 'Marcuse called out the nonsense of the philosopheme, that one could even inwardly accept or reject torture' (GS 11 p. 413). The increased focus on freedom of the will arises at a specific moment in the development of modern bourgeois society, namely when the idea of universal determinism becomes central to the sciences, and the idea of the individual's will as self-determining is valorized in a way which is not present in the ancient world and in feudalism. While concern with freedom is present in many aspects of the history of Western philosophy, the 'concept of the will itself...as concept of the alternative: freedom or unfreedom of the will, only belongs to a relatively late phase of philosophical reflection'. As he says of Kant: 'it never occurred to him whether freedom itself, which is an eternal idea to him, could be historical, not just as a concept but in terms of its content of experience. Whole epochs, whole societies did not only lack the concept but the thing as well' (GS 6 p. 218). The modern idea of freedom cannot be thought of in separation from its political and historical contexts: the 'objective' social realm therefore is part of what is often seen as essentially interior to the subject.

Philosophy's relationship to freedom can itself fall prey to a further dialectic: 'The more the theory urges freedom, the more the theory insists that human beings are free in themselves, that their will is absolutely free, that they are absolutely responsible for themselves, the more the theory lends itself to repression'. In structurally unequal economic circumstances, freedom is often invoked to justify inequality, on the grounds that everyone can supposedly work their way out of poverty. Such concrete instantiations of the issue are a further reason why Adorno is concerned at how the law can create injustice by the 'formal principle of equivalence'. Moreover, couching the issue of freedom in terms of a metaphysical absolute leaves one with no way of understanding the role freedom plays in the history which leads to the Holocaust: *why* does supposed human autonomy lead to repression and blind obedience? Despite his objections to how Hegel sees the law, Adorno concurs with his understanding of freedom as inseparable from human institutions. Hegel shows how 'freedom, which appears to us as if it were just a quality of subjectivity, as if its possibility could only be decided and judged in the subjective realm', actually depends 'on the objective, on the extent to which we are capable at all, via what we do as subjectively formally free beings, of influencing overwhelmingly structured institutional reality'.

In Adorno's sometimes hyperbolic view of the 'totality' of modern society, in the wake of the Holocaust, individual freedom has largely become a delusion that was destroyed by the structures which dominate the modern world. As he says in *The Authoritarian Personality*: 'The more our society tends to become "integral," i.e., a thoroughly organized totality, the more the pressure increases that it exercises upon the comparatively impotent individual'. This process has been part of the development of modern capitalism at least since the 19th century: the crucial aspect of the process is that the actions of individuals bring about a system in which what those individuals intend has little bearing on what actually results from the system. What Adorno often refers to as the 'context of delusion'—the world constituted through the system of commodity exchange—is a further example of why he thinks conceptions of subjective and objective have to be rethought.

The autonomy of the individual is, then, so tied up with a system that what can appear to the individual as the exercise of freedom can actually be the product of determining factors of which they are not aware. Certain 21st-century concerns can illustrate the point. The projection onto others of poor white people's real suffering and frustration often takes the form of a racism that makes them unable to realize that they are part of an economic and political system which has systematically impoverished them for decades. Focusing on the metaphysical question of whether such people have free will, when they have little or no space for self-determination, further underlines how freedom cannot be reduced to being something that resides solely in the subject. The modern concern with freedom itself derives from changes in the economic and social constitution of the objective social world, like the rise of bourgeois individualism, that happen independently of the will of individuals, so that 'one could say that in a very real sense freedom gets mixed up in the context of determination'.

Moral life and the 'additional factor'

If Adorno's points are taken seriously, the way philosophical discussion about ethics is often carried out can appear to be inadequate. If 'there is no right life in life that is wrong', people may be confronted with situations where there is no 'right' course of action, because whatever they do may just perpetuate unjust social conditions. The choice between 'consequentialist' theories that focus on the results of an action as what gives it its moral worth, and 'deontological' theories that judge actions in terms of their accordance with norms, like duty, can look abstract in relation to the reality of moral situations in a world where so much is dominated by systemic pressures: 'Freedom . . . necessarily presupposes the freedom of the whole, and cannot, as isolated freedom, thus without the freedom of the whole of society, even be thought'. As such: 'the reason why the question of moral philosophy has become so problematic today is primarily that the substantiality of ethics, thus the possibility that a right way of living was already given and present in the forms in which the community exists, has become radically obsolete'. But what, given the fact that the 'freedom of the whole of society' is conspicuously absent, does Adorno propose with respect to how we should respond to modern moral dilemmas?

Adorno does not think we can just abandon the usual concerns of moral philosophy, but the philosopher who proposes a moral theory has always to keep in mind the fallibility that results from their location in circumstances that are not wholly transparent to them. His concern is to show up the limits of theorizing about freedom and morality in relation to the reality of moral life, in order to avoid philosophy conspiring with self-deception. He criticizes the kind of thinking about freedom often encountered in analytical philosophy, which can lead to the following: 'In order conclusively, so to speak empirically, to make a decision on whether the will is free, situations have to be rigorously purged of their empirical content; thought-experimental conditions must be produced in which as few determinants as possible are noticeable' (GS 6 p. 223). The 'trolley problem' is a familiar example of this: would you switch the track for a runaway railway trolley that would kill five people to a track that would kill just one person? What if stopping the trolley killing the five could be achieved by pushing a fat man off a bridge onto the line? The point is that nobody knows what they would do in such an—already highly unlikely—situation because one does not know what else would be affecting one in the decision. Adorno, in contrast, cites empirical cases from history and literature that can be interpreted in differing ways to show why thought experiments cannot grasp the reality of moral life. The result is not a theoretical account of how to make moral decisions: the focus is instead on showing the contradictions involved in real dilemmas, in order not to exclude the contingencies they inevitably involve. He sums this up in the assertion that 'It cannot be prophesied, even of the most morally upright person how they would behave under torture'.

This sort of approach might seem likely to paralyse any attempt to act, given that people will always be faced with contradictions which may not be able to be resolved by a decision to act. Hamlet beckons, as Adorno himself suggests. Action, rather than mere conditioned or unreflective behaviour, seems to involve some kind of reconciliation between a person's impulses and social norms: 'the subject only knows itself to be free to the extent that its action appears identical with it, and that is only the case with things that are conscious'. However, just adhering to a norm is no guarantee that one will, in concrete circumstances, actually act in terms of it. For this to happen, something that is not given with the norm itself has to come into play, which he terms 'the additional factor', '*das Hinzutretende*': 'people suffer from their knowledge, because they have the experience that there is no longer a direct way into practice from this knowledge, but that one needs a third thing, precisely that element of irrationality, of what is not purely reducible to reason'. He tells of meeting one of the surviving members of the 20 July plot to assassinate Hitler. The plotters had to ponder the terrible consequences for themselves of failure, the possibility that what they intended doing might make things even worse, the threat to their relatives in the event of failure, and a host of other factors. The survivor makes it clear that the situation in relation to Hitler was so 'unbearable' that they felt compelled to act, but not for clearly formulated reasons. Rather, there was, Adorno contends, a 'moment of irrationality', that is essentially a-theoretical, which made them act.

The 'additional factor' cannot be subsumed into norm-based moral reflection: it therefore involves a connection between nature and freedom. For Kant morality depends on the ability to resist natural impulses, and for Hegel on the reconciliation of our natural and our social being. Adorno, in contrast, wants to include the possibility of natural impulses being part of the reality of moral life: 'Impulse, which is both intramental and somatic, drives beyond the sphere of consciousness, to which it still also belongs. With it freedom reaches into experience' (GS 6 p. 228), and we are 'capable, by dint of this impulse, of getting into, leaping into, going into the objective sphere which is otherwise obstructed for us by our own rationality'.

By trying to account for freedom in terms of the nature of human impulses, Adorno suggests he will be accused of invoking 'something merely determined'. In order to respond to the fact that impulses can also be merely irrational causes of our actions, as well as part of freedom, Adorno develops a dialectical approach to freedom and nature, using aspects of psychoanalysis. We have already encountered the basic pattern of thought. In order to gain control of nature, the subject has to control its own impulses, which are part of its nature, and this gives rise to a contradiction: 'whilst it is only with the development of consciousness at all that something like freedom becomes possible, at the same time it is the development of consciousness that pushes freedom back into this archaic-mimetic moment that is essential to it'. Whereas Kant largely sees freedom in terms of opposition to somatic impulses, Adorno thinks this can be mere repression, and that real freedom would come from finding ways to allow these impulses to gain expression without being harmful. This cannot be achieved simply by the establishing of norms, because in any real situation there will be conflicts between norms that lead precisely to the situation that involves the 'additional factor'. Norms, as we saw with respect to the law, can also become repressive by rigid application.

A new categorical imperative

So how does Adorno conceive of a grounding of ethics? Kant famously seeks to do this on the basis of the 'categorical imperative', one formulation of which is: 'I ought never to act except in such a way *that I can also will that my maxim should become a universal law*'. Adorno does not deny that some sense of conscience is part of our make-up as social beings, and Kant is relying on this to arrive at his imperative. However, conscience depends on norms that have arisen in a world of distorted social relations, and can, as Adolph Eichmann showed, be turned into forms of adherence to duty that are used to legitimize barbarism. Adorno argues that 'All the concepts in honour of freedom which are supposed in the *Critique of Practical Reason* to fill out the gulf between the imperative and people are repressive: law, compulsion, deference, duty. Causality from freedom corrupts the latter into obedience' (GS 6 p. 231). A search for a universal foundation relies on reference to a single grounding principle, like Kant's universalization of maxims for action via the categorical imperative, but actual moral decisions generally involve competing imperatives. Kant's absolute prohibition on lying comes up, for instance, as the novelist and political writer Benjamin Constant (1767–1830) pointed out, against the situation where lying might save people's lives. Lying might actually in some cases lead to something worse than what it tries to prevent, but there is no sure way of knowing this, and Kant's strict separation of empirical and moral aspects of the dilemma does nothing to help here.

Such dilemmas mean Adorno insists that moral justification has to respond to empirical historical contingency, and this leads to his own version of a categorical imperative:

> Hitler enforced a new categorical imperative on humankind in the state of unfreedom: to organise their thinking and action in such a way that Auschwitz does not repeat itself, that nothing similar should happen. This imperative is just as resistant to being given a grounding as in its time the givenness of Kant's imperative. (GS 6 p. 358)

He claims that Kant just 'breaks off' the philosophical argument by seeing the moral law as 'given', rather than argued for, and this again suggests that 'right action is not to be purely resolved into theoretical requirements'. It is, then, crucial to see how individual moral life is subject to pressures from a collectively constituted social, economic, and political world that sets the frame of the individual's scope for action, and so can erode their ability to judge. The primacy of the objective social whole in relation to the subject is, he thinks, unavoidable. This entails an 'objective theory of society', where 'the supposed facts of conscious and unconscious modes of behaviour of subjects are in many ways something derivative. The essential object of knowledge of society is its objective context, its structural laws which individual human beings obey even in their forms of reaction' (GS 11 p. 42).

Adorno is therefore concerned to warn against moral certainty, and advocates 'learning in reflection on one's own having been

Theodor W. Adorno

conditioned [*Bedingtheit*] to also allow legitimacy to what is different and to feel that the true injustice is really always there where one assumes one is right and the other is wrong'. He sums this approach up as follows: 'Moral certainty does not exist; to imply that it does is already immoral, a false exoneration of the individual from whatever might be termed ethical life' (GS 6 p. 241). The ways in which modern societies are organized mean that individual action is always likely to result in something unintended of which the individual could not be aware.

This might seem a rather feeble way for Adorno to advocate his categorical imperative to think and act such that nothing like Auschwitz could be repeated. However, he also makes it clear that after Auschwitz 'we might not know what is the absolute good, the absolute norm, or even only what man or the human or humanity is, but we very well know what the inhuman is' (GS 6 p. 261). The question is why modern societies are able to make their members oblivious to the inhuman, as is still apparent, for example, in the widespread antagonism in the contemporary world to the sufferings of refugees and racially oppressed people. Such antagonism is precisely linked to a moral narcissism that tries to blame such people for their own oppression, while relying on the sense that one's own life is not morally questionable. In the UK this often takes the form of a refusal to look at the genocidal history of the British Empire that is still a major factor in enforced migration, and this refusal is often accompanied by the contention that other countries' history is just as murderous, as though this makes British history any less so.

Adorno's insistence on the empirical, historical aspect of thinking about freedom results from his conviction that understanding modern moral life is tied up with social, economic, and political pressures that cannot be understood from the perspective of the isolated individual moral subject. Perhaps most importantly, he focuses on *how* modern culture can make people unable to see the reality of what they are doing and what they are involved in. His repeated target here is conformism, and the crucial issue is how the power of conformism comes about. In an era which can produce the likes of Bolsonaro, Orban, Modi, Trump, and other authoritarian politicians, Adorno's—sometimes flawed—analyses of the functioning of conformism in culture deserve renewed attention, as we will see in the next chapter.

Chapter 5
The culture industry

Total social delusion?

When writing about the 'culture industry' in *DE*, Adorno and Horkheimer originally referred to 'mass culture', but they decided to replace the term because it could too easily sound like 'culture that spontaneously emerged from the masses, the contemporary form of folk art' (GS 10.1 p. 337). Instead, they contend that the culture industry produces culture as a commodity like any other, in line with the view of modern industry as standardized production which they associated with Kant's schematism. Adorno's view of the culture industry is, however, not unproblematic, and this is suggested, for example, by a statement like the following: 'The total context of the culture industry, which leaves nothing out, is one with total social delusion' (GS 4 p. 235). But how, if social delusion is total, can anyone know that it is delusion at all? Logically there is no way out of this situation, so one has to assume Adorno is exaggerating.

In 'What is coming to terms with the past?', referring to the persistence in the Federal Republic of the kind of socio-political and economic factors that led to Nazism, he says: 'I have exaggerated the gloomy side of things, following the maxim that today only exaggeration can be the medium of truth' (GS 10.2 p. 568). He seeks to justify such a stance in an essay on 'Opinion

Delusion Society', citing the case of a pedestrian wondering whether to cross the road when the lights have changed to yellow. On the assumption that the person cannot rely on the next car not being driven by someone reckless, even if it turns out that they are actually a considerate driver, the rational thing to do is not to take the real risk of being killed. In doing so, the person exaggerates by making the worst case scenario the basis of not crossing: 'All thinking is exaggeration, insofar as every thought that really is a thought overshoots its fulfilment by given facts. The potential for truth as well as the potential for delusion nests in this difference between thought and fulfilment' (GS 10.2 p. 577). Despite this defence of exaggeration, the way in which Adorno presents his analysis of the culture industry does weaken what he has to say. At the same time, some of the evidently problematic things he says about specific aspects of modern culture, like jazz, eventually come to apply to other aspects of the music industry, such as the worst kinds of industry-produced pop music. If Adorno's exaggerations are read just as warnings of where things can go if we fail to look beyond the immediate facts, his account of the culture industry does offer resources, not least for understanding the widespread contemporary success of reactionary political forces in the USA, the UK, and elsewhere.

Adorno proposes an essential connection between the culture industry and the functioning of capitalist societies: 'Amusement is the extension of work in late capitalism. It is sought by those who wish to escape the mechanised process of labour, in order to be able to cope with it anew' (GS 3 p. 159). It has been argued that one reason the US working-class rarely became widely radicalized after the First World War, despite their frequently dire situation, was because the 'American Dream' was kept alive by the 'dream factory' of Hollywood, which distracted working people from the reality of their situation. Writing in the 1940s, Adorno does not fully subscribe to this view, as he thinks the development of new forms of communication means people will be less likely to be taken in by consoling ideological products like Hollywood movies.

In *DE* he claims: 'The atrophy of imagination and spontaneity of the consumer of culture today does not need first to be reduced to psychological mechanisms. The products themselves, above all the most characteristic, the talkie, paralyse those capacities by their objective constitution' (GS 3 p. 148). This latter remark introduces a further debatable element of Adorno's thinking about culture. He looks at cultural products in terms of the interpretation and critical analysis of the product itself, which he terms 'content analysis', rather than primarily in terms of the actual reception and effects of the products on their recipients. The danger here is that the focus on the analysable aspects of a cultural artefact may tell us little about its effect on people in real situations. This danger results from the idea of 'total' delusion. If that is presupposed, focus on reception loses much of its point: attention will be directed instead to what does the deluding. Whether it in fact deludes cannot, however, be established in this way. Adorno seems at times, then, to see the dialectic between production and reception in culture in too one-sided a fashion. However, as we shall see later, when he does detailed empirical research on production and reception of cultural phenomena, some of the results are more plausible.

The exclusion of the new

So what are the characteristics of the industry that create conformism? The following is exaggerated, but the history of Hollywood (Figure 4) and of other aspects of popular culture does confirm at least some of the diagnosis:

> What is new in the mass cultural phase as compared to the late liberal phase is the exclusion of the new. The machine revolves in the same place. While it already determines consumption, it excludes what is untested as a risk. The film people look suspiciously at every manuscript that is not already reassuringly based on a bestseller. That is why the talk is always of idea, novelty and surprise, of that which is at the same time all too familiar and unprecedented. (GS 3 p. 156)

4. Hollywood.

Why does Adorno attach so much weight to the absence of 'the new'? His core assumption is that the state of Western society of that time—which then improved after the war, but has arguably again slipped back—is fundamentally unjust and repressive. In an unjust society culture that is worthy of the name would enable questioning of that society, which means people will be confronted with perhaps disturbing new ideas and ways of responding to the world. In contrast, the use of modern technology in the culture industry is in the name of the economic status quo: 'the thought of "exhausting" given technical possibilities, the full utilisation of capacities for aesthetic mass consumption, belongs to the economic system, which refuses to use the capacities where it is about the abolition of hunger' (GS 3 p. 162).

Aesthetic mass consumption, then, encourages conformism that sustains oppression by obscuring the fact that oppression could be overcome. In a later account of his reflections on the culture industry, Adorno claims:

The overall effect of the culture industry is that of an anti-Enlightenment; in it…Enlightenment, the progressive technical mastery of nature, becomes mass deception, a means of fettering consciousness. It prevents the formation of autonomous, independent, consciously judging and deciding individuals. They, however, would be the prerequisite for a democratic society, which can only be maintained and developed in mature individuals. (GS 10.1 p. 345)

This once again involves the 'primacy of the objective': systemic factors prevent the development of individual resistance to 'life that is wrong'. When discussing the complexity of serious modern music, Adorno argues that

The contemporary inability of the masses to understand anything complicated, which is inherited from their being excluded from education [*Bildung*, which in German has a wider sense of initiation into all aspects of culture] is intensified today by the culture industry, which shapes them, and by their own mechanisation in the labour process. In their so-called free time, they are hardly able to grasp anything which does not resemble this labour process. (GS 14 p. 59)

When applied to some of what, both in Adorno's time and now, is produced in popular films and TV, such a judgement has some justification, and the nature of politics is clearly affected by this. However, Adorno also says much the same about most forms of music apart from the music he regards as articulating the truth of the historical situation: the case of jazz will highlight his underestimation of the difficulty of this kind of analysis.

Consider, then, the essential premises of Adorno's analysis. He regards the culture industry as functioning in a different way from previous forms of ideology. Following Marx, ideology is 'socially conditioned false consciousness', and the new situation is that ideology, unlike in earlier forms of capitalism:

by no means blindly, anonymously crystallises itself from the social process, but is scientifically tailored to society. This is done with the products of the culture industry, film, magazines, illustrated newspapers, radio, bestselling literature of the most varied types, among which novel-biographies play their special role, and now, in America, especially television. (GS 8 p. 475)

The ideology of 19th-century capitalism arose from the pressures of industrialization, in a 'world which was largely dominated by economic laws which enforced themselves above the heads of people' (GS 8 p. 483). The rapidity and brutality of this process is well analysed in Karl Polanyi's *The Great Transformation*, first published in 1944, the same year as *DE*. Polanyi states, in terms which echo Adorno's view of the 'exchange principle':

All transactions are turned into money transactions, and these in turn require that a medium of exchange be introduced into every articulation of industrial life. All incomes must derive from the sale of something or other, and whatever the actual source of a person's income, it must be regarded as resulting from sale.

In the later form of capitalism the culture industry researches how to produce the culture that will be effective in keeping people reconciled to a society governed by the exchange principle.

The consumers of this culture are seen as having to conform to a labour process which hinders their self-realization by leaving little space or time for it. The ideology of the culture industry is 'intensifying duplication and justification of the situation that exists anyway' (GS 8 p. 477), leaving no opportunity for developing non-commodified forms of social and economic life. The rapid move away from traditional religious authority that accompanies the growth of capitalism means that autonomy has little chance to develop: 'the authority of the Bible is replaced by the authority of the sports field, television, and "true stories", which are based on the claim of the literal, of reality on this side of the productive imagination' (GS 8 p. 99). This sort of analysis is clearly very compressed, and does not cover everything that is at issue. Adorno does address a key further ideological product of modern capitalism, namely nationalism, although he thinks its role in 'late capitalism', that is capitalism dominated by technologically advanced transnational corporations, is in certain respects diminished. Given recent history, this assessment may need some revision, as is shown by the encouragement of nationalism by those who seek to shore up the collapsing economic model of neoliberalism.

Jazz

Adorno's interpretation of all forms of US popular culture of the time as means of cementing conformism raises some fundamental questions. This is where the example of jazz is significant, because it does not fit well into Adorno's approach. There is a paradigmatic mismatch between his overall theoretical frame, and the empirical evidence concerning a supposed manifestation of the culture industry. It is therefore worth considering the issue in a bit of detail. Adorno's essay 'On Jazz', the first piece he wrote on the topic, is from 1936, before he went to the USA, so it was based on recordings, sheet music, and whatever he may have heard in Europe that was called jazz. The lack of detail to back up his case could be seen as a result of his contingent circumstances at the time. However, he refers to the jazz essay even in his work in the 1960s, though by that time his view was sometimes more differentiated. Core ideas of the essay are also carried over into the analyses of the culture industry in *DE*, and elsewhere.

Adorno's later use of his 1936 analysis is already put in question by the fact that, even by 1944, jazz had radically changed from the jazz referred to in the essay. The 'bebop revolution' of the 1940s was a reaction against commercially promoted swing music, which was in effect the pop music of the time and is in some of its manifestations the justified target of Adorno's criticisms.

The progenitors of bebop were mainly black musicians, and the increased technical demands of the music were not least intended as a means of excluding musicians who just followed the commercialized vein of swing. The pursuit of a new jazz vocabulary in bebop also involved an element of political protest against a dominant white culture. Bebop's extension of harmonic, melodic, and rhythmic vocabulary lays the foundations of jazz's continual revision and questioning of received musical assumptions and practices that continues to this day.

Even before bebop, jazz had, through figures like Louis Armstrong, begun to help establish a specifically black urban culture that generated resistance to white domination. In the jazz essay Adorno insists, though, that 'this much is certain, that the serviceability of jazz does not negate alienation, but amplifies it. Jazz is a commodity in the strict sense, it is subject to the laws, and the contingency of the market' (GS 17 p. 78). Insofar as everything is affected by those laws and that contingency, this is, of course, necessarily the case. However, the fact that from the early 1940s probably the most important development in jazz history was a reaction against what was dominating the market, and many of Charlie Parker's (eventually) most influential recordings were made on obscure, commercially unsuccessful labels, suggests Adorno neglects the dialectic involved in the commodification of jazz. It is precisely when jazz became more assimilated into the mass market that it produced some of its most important music as a reaction *against* that assimilation. In this sense, jazz does precisely what Adorno, as we shall see, demands of 'new music'.

Jazz has been involved from its beginnings in a negotiation and confrontation with musical and social conformity. One just needs to read some of the negative reactions to jazz from the white culture of the time (and since) to see this. Adorno, though, sees the unconventional elements of jazz, not as expressing protest, but as identification with the oppressor: 'They characterise a subjectivity which protests against a collective power which it itself "is"; for this reason its protest appears ridiculous and is beaten down by the drum, like syncopation is by the beat' (GS 17 p. 100). His assessment of jazz rhythm changes somewhat later in his career: in 1962 he says, for example, that jazz 'taught technical skill, quick-wittedness, the concentration which had otherwise been degraded by light music, also tonal and rhythmic capacity for differentiation' (GS 14 pp. 212–13). Elsewhere, discussing how to sustain rhythmic differentiation in music performance, he remarks: 'A light falls from here on a real function of jazz: namely to sustain such differentiations, which otherwise are disappearing. As, by the way, *interpretation* has a lot to learn from jazz'.

What many see as a key aspect of jazz, though, he dismisses both in 1936 and often thereafter: 'the much cited improvisations, those hot-passages and breaks have merely ornamental significance, never constructive and form-establishing significance' (GS 17 p. 82). However, even around 1936, extended improvisation had begun to develop, in ways which come to full 'form-establishing' fruition in jazz from the 1940s and 1950s onwards. Adorno also fails to see that jazz improvisation lives from communication with a live audience, who can effectively become part of the band, rather than being passive consumers of a product. When talking about how to develop adequate theories concerning an area of research, Adorno often advocates 'unrestricted experience', remaining open to what might be distorted by the frame in which the research is carried out. In writing about jazz, he largely fails to follow his own avowed intentions.

In the context of his assessment of the culture industry—and this is the key wider point that affects other aspects of his work—his view of jazz seems to derive from what could be termed a 'Gnostic' attitude, which creates a radical separation between what is free of delusion and what isn't. In these terms anything involved with the exchange principle and the market necessarily contributes to the context of delusion, rather than making more sense of the world. This attitude results from the way he sometimes prioritizes objective structural factors in society over detailed empirical investigation of the ways people may resist delusion.

Adorno's failure with respect to jazz also results from a neglect of how musical practices cannot just be understood by 'content analysis' of musical works. In much of his writing on the arts Adorno seeks to avoid the consigning of all judgements on aesthetic and cultural matters to the realm of the 'merely subjective'. He does this in the name of 'social theory by dint of the explication of aesthetic right and wrong in the heart of the musical objects' (GS 17 p. 33). This involves:

> comprehending and analysing subjective responses towards music in relation to the thing itself [*zur Sache selbst*] and its determinable content, rather than ignoring the quality of the object, treating it as a mere stimulus of projections and limiting oneself to the identification, measuring and ordering of subjective reactions or of sedimented responses to music. (GS 14 pp. 176–7)

This approach, which rightly questions the reduction of aesthetic appreciation to psychologically establishable facts that pay no heed to the aesthetic constitution of the work responded to—its 'content'—is of undoubted value. The problems with the approach derive from its focusing too exclusively on musical analysis of 'objective' factors, and from the assumption that the subjects involved have been wholly assimilated into the context of delusion. Adorno relies on an objectifying, observational perspective, which he argues for as follows: 'art cannot absolve itself of the discipline of science, from which it borrows, with whatever right it does so, its ideal of objectivity' (GS 16 p. 528). What is missing is a reflection on how to understand the dimensions of art which involve *participation* in a practice—which relates to what happens, for example, in participation in a ritual—without which the art in question makes no sense.

5. Adorno.

Jazz is a form of expressive sociality, where the music develops through the practice of dialogue within the band, between musicians, and with the audience. Adorno (Figure 5), as we saw, appreciates the problem of how to characterize the relationship between subjective and objective when he talks about issues in philosophy. He seems, though, blind to the interactions between subjective and objective involved in the history of jazz. Jazz is demonstrably critical of the racist and exploitative society in which it emerged, in ways that become inexplicable in the terms of Adorno's analysis of the culture industry. Innovators in jazz, like John Coltrane or Ornette Coleman, often faced intense resistance even within the jazz community, before what they did came to be appreciated. In this respect they do not differ from composers such as Berg, Schoenberg, and Webern, whom Adorno sees as the paradigm of how modern art should function. Like all art, jazz produces conventions that can become rigidified, but opposing convention is precisely the motor that has kept jazz—which Adorno in 1936 declared 'beyond salvation' (GS 17 p. 101)—alive today.

The difficulties in Adorno's account of how modern culture comes to be dominated by forces of conformity point to a series of issues in relation to philosophical understanding of modern societies. There is here a tension between investigation of the way objective, structural factors determine the actions of social subjects, and the need to show how resistance to those factors is empirically manifested in what subjects do in concrete social situations. This tension cannot be definitively resolved, as Adorno's own dialectical reflections on subjective and objective suggest, and has to be taken into account in any specific investigation of cultural phenomena. Despite the criticisms I have detailed, Adorno himself, like other members of the Frankfurt School, cannot be accused of failing to do empirical research. From the investigations of *The Authoritarian Personality*, to research on astrology in newspapers in Los Angeles, to studies of the functioning of local government in Bielefeld, and other projects, he often engaged in study of the detail of social phenomena. We touched on the decisive issue in this context when considering exaggeration: how is one to go beyond empirical data to understand the context which informs those data? In short, what role do data and theory play for Adorno in understanding society?

Chapter 6
Society

Theory in the sciences

Not many years ago the idea that, both in the USA and Europe, political movements involving varying degrees of fascism would gain considerable voter support in many Western countries, and come to power in some, would have seemed quite outlandish. Adorno, of course, would have found nothing outlandish about this, as his view of the persistence of what made fascism possible makes clear. So what is it about his theory of modern society that made him turn out to be prescient? A conference in 1961, at Tübingen University, of the German Society for Sociology was the beginning of an influential debate on the methodology of the social sciences that involved Adorno, Karl Popper, Jürgen Habermas, Hans Albert, Ralf Dahrendorf, and other philosophers and social and political scientists, which came to be known as 'The Positivism Debate in German Sociology'. The label 'positivism' in this context is actually more trouble than it is worth, because it has too many (sometimes conflicting) meanings, and Popper, for example, whom Adorno put in the category, objected to being included. Rather than get entangled in discussing the disputed definition of 'positivism' it is best to concentrate on the substance of the debate. This concerned the relationship between the natural sciences and the social sciences, and the status of their respective theoretical claims. Related debates had been part of the German academic landscape since the second half of the 19th century, centring around the idea that the natural sciences were concerned with establishing causal laws, while the humanities were concerned with the understanding of unique human phenomena. The question was whether the latter had any kind of scientific status, given that it concerned subjects with some capacity for self-determination, rather than law-bound natural objects.

In his main contribution to the debate Adorno states: 'Cognition [*Erkenntnis*, which also has the sense of 'insight' and 'recognition'] is, and by no means by accident, exaggeration. For just as little as any single thing is "true", but by dint of its mediation always also its own other, the whole is in turn just as little true' (GS 8 p. 319). Adorno, as we have seen, adopts the Hegelian idea that the truth about things emerges from the analysis of their relationships to other things in a totality. He at the same time adheres to the anti-Hegelian idea that, rather than this totality itself being 'the true', it is a context of delusion. Investigation of social phenomena therefore has to move beyond—hence, as we saw, 'exaggeration'—immediate data, such as interviews with people involved in a social issue, to what objectively influences the interview responses that is not apparent in the responses themselves. Hence also the difficulty of such investigation, because the effects of the social context result from systemic factors which are not transparent to those within the system.

The untruth of the whole presumably also distorts the responses of those within the whole who seek to understand it. Adorno is therefore careful not to claim that his approach can know what undistorted relations would be, which would require an extra-mundane perspective. At the same time, there is no doubt about what massively distorted relations are: Auschwitz makes this much clear, and the paucity of means within society to resist what can lead again to such catastrophe is the basis of how he sees modern society. Only by seeking out large-scale tendencies that are not immediately apparent in the data can the signs of impending danger be made accessible. Whatever may be questionable in Adorno's approach, the warnings it contains cannot be conjured away, as recent history is showing.

Adorno makes the source of the dispute, and what he means by 'positivism' clearer when he states that 'Positivism regards sociology as one science among others, and, since Comte, regards the tested methods of the older sciences, especially the natural sciences, as transferrable to sociology' (GS 8 p. 316). The key elements of the debate have to do with how the notion of objectivity is conceived, and with the relationship between facts and values. In sociology the concern with values is particularly associated with Max Weber's insistence on 'value-freedom' in all the sciences. In his remarks on this issue Weber is often specifically concerned with teachers not imposing their evaluations on their students, and this points to the essential difficulty that concerns Adorno.

The data of social science often consist of people's views of themselves and of the society they inhabit. As such, they involve 'subjective' evaluations, to which people have an obvious right, whence Weber's concern with the teacher–student relationship, where there is an inherent power imbalance. At the same time, evaluations must be open to questioning: is the racist entitled to a free pass, because they sincerely hold their racist views, based on whatever their 'values' are? How, though, is such questioning to take place? As anyone active on social media knows, just proving that the factual aspects of what someone believes are false generally has little effect, because what people invest in derives from a longer, affectively charged history which shapes their view of the world in ways that are very hard to shift. To take a recent extreme example:

> Emergency room patients in the USA often don't want to believe
> Covid-19 is real even after testing positive for the virus, according to

a South Dakota nurse: 'they don't want to believe that Covid is real...their last dying words are, "This can't be happening, it's not real"'.

(Similar incidents were subsequently reported in the UK.) The values and convictions which inform people's views of the world have an objective aspect that is open to critical exploration of their development, and which the people concerned may not be aware of. Adorno talks in this sense of 'the sheer impossibility of explaining psychologically what does not arise from the inner life of individual people' (GS 8 p. 51). The Covid patients' convictions are, in these terms, generated by systemic distortions, for example occasioned by the media, which derive from the failure to sustain a functioning social whole that inspires trust in its members.

The basis of Adorno's approach is summed up as follows: 'The social veil is constituted by the fact that social tendencies assert themselves over the heads of people, that they do not know those tendencies as their own' (GS 8 p. 54). Moving the veil aside is difficult because the analysis tells people things which contradict what they themselves see as their relationship to the society they inhabit. Adorno often uses psychoanalysis as a model for this situation, because it argues that many actions are motivated by unconscious factors which may not enter the mind of the subject performing the action. The key link here is Freud's super-ego, 'conscience'—'the social instance of control in the individual' (GS 3 p. 229)—which is formed through internalization of parental and social norms which precede the individual subject. The externally instituted super-ego draws its power from repressed drives in the id which the subject feels as its own, even though the norms it internalizes actually derive from society.

The scientific status of psychoanalysis has always been disputed, and Adorno discusses this issue at various points in relation to sociological research, such as that presented in *The Authoritarian*

Personality. He maintains that psychoanalysis, despite being largely ignored by other sciences—and particularly psychiatry—

> provided hypotheses that were practically viable within the science to explain what was otherwise inexplicable, namely that the overwhelming majority of people puts up with relations of dominance, identifies with them, and is induced by them to adopt irrational attitudes whose opposition to the most simple interests of their self-preservation is completely obvious. (GS 8 pp. 331–2)

The echoes of contemporary politics, in cases such as the UK's leaving the European Union ('Brexit'), whose worst effects will arguably be felt by many people who voted for it and continue to support it against all the evidence, and poor white people voting for an American president who gives massive tax cuts to billionaires while blocking the introduction of universal healthcare, suggest the continuing importance of Adorno's approach.

Adorno is, then, concerned with the justification of methods in social research, given the demand for it to be 'scientific'. The original aim of psychoanalysis was to produce general psychological laws, but Adorno sees it as its most productive via 'immersion in the detail' of a relatively small number of specific cases, rather than via large-scale surveys that result in inductive hypotheses in the manner of the physical sciences. Talking of *The Authoritarian Personality*, which used techniques from empirical sociology, like questionnaires and interviews, to investigate post-war Americans' susceptibility to fascism, Adorno maintains:

> that the book not only encouraged but also changed the direction of empirical research to some extent, lies in the fact that it produced a concrete relationship between the complex of a social psychology oriented towards Freud and empirical methods of research. Not that it presumed to prove or disprove Freud empirically. (GS 8 pp. 542–3)

Society

The concern here, beyond what was specifically at issue in the Positivism Debate—some of which now appears rather outdated—is 'scientism', the assumption that the theories and methods of the natural sciences should apply to all disciplines, including the humanities and social sciences.

What status does 'theory' with respect to the social sciences have if it does not use the methods of the natural sciences? Adorno maintains that 'there are object domains in which reality cannot at all be appropriately captured with the norms established by the sciences'. The data for the physical sciences are 'as lacking in qualities as possible, not in themselves already preformed, not in themselves objectively qualified ... smallest units or elements'. The units or elements of social theories, in contrast, are individual subjects with complex life histories of the kind dealt with in psychoanalysis. In consequence, stripping the qualitative aspects away in order to arrive at quantifiable data derived from survey questionnaires, etc., that can be analysed using quantitative methods is likely to strip away much of what is essential to understanding a society. An indeterminate amount of factual data can be collected in a society, but much of it may tell one nothing about how that society actually functions. Moreover, choosing which data to analyse necessarily involves evaluation of the kind which value-freedom is supposed to exclude. Adorno's objection to what he sees as 'positivist' sociology is that

> In at least a very considerable sector of its activity it is based on opinions, behaviour, the self-understanding of individual subjects and of society, rather than on the latter. In such a conception, society is to a large extent the statistically determined, average consciousness or unconsciousness of socialised and socially acting subjects, not the medium in which they move. (GS 8 pp. 287–8)

So how is one to gain access to the 'medium' that society is beyond what is accessed by conventional sociology? Instead of 'traditional theory', one here needs to engage in 'critical theory', the term

Theodor W. Adorno

which is associated with the work of the 'Frankfurt School' of
social research as a whole.

Critical theory

The differentiation of kinds of theory can best be understood
in terms we have already explored: the key is again
relationships between subject and object. 'Traditional theory',
'positivism', 'scientism', etc. 'treats society, which is potentially
the self-determining subject, without further ado as if it were an
object to be determined from outside' (GS 8 p. 317). Society is only
potentially a subject: in its present state society functions as
something objective that 'stands against' individual subjects. One
therefore has to see it in dialectical terms: subjective and objective
can only be grasped via changing social relations. Critical theory
'orients itself, despite all experience of reification . . . by . . . the idea
of society as subject' (GS 8 p. 317). Given that society is not yet
'subject' in this sense, being instead determined by objective
forces 'over the heads of people'—hence its reified 'thing-like'
nature—there is a contradiction between two senses of society.
Just gathering ever more data about society as it is in its reified
state can reinforce the status quo.

What is the aim of social research, if it is not to better society?
Popper sees social research in terms of individual social problems
that should be addressed by 'piecemeal social engineering' that
avoids 'Utopian social engineering', which he associates with the
disasters of totalitarian and authoritarian attempts to impose
social change. Adorno, who is equally concerned at how social
change can become the opposite of what its progenitors may
intend, thinks, though, that piecemeal analysis of social problems
is not sufficient, and must be complemented by the attempt to
grasp the wider context and source of the problems:

> Society only becomes a problem, in Popper's language, to someone
> who can think of it as different to society as it exists now; only

through what it is not will it reveal itself as what it is, and that is what a sociology would need to do which does not, as admittedly the majority of its projects do, limit itself to the purposes of public and private administration. (GS 8 p. 564)

The wider context is the 'totality', which is not immediately apparent in the particular instances. However, 'the supremacy of the whole, which is admittedly abstract, but in a certain sense also eludes the universal concept, can only be encountered in the experience of the particular and in the interpretation of this experience of the particular' (GS 8 p. 587). The totality itself cannot, then, directly be an object of investigation: 'No experiment could conclusively explain the dependence of every social phenomenon on the totality, because the whole, that preforms the concrete phenomena, itself never enters particular experimental set-ups' (GS 8 p. 556). So how does the totality play a role in social research at all? We just saw that Adorno insists that the totality is 'encountered in the experience of the particular': it is, therefore, 'not an affirmative, but rather a critical category. Dialectical criticism seeks to salvage or to help to produce what does not obey the totality, what resists it' (GS 8 p. 292). This idea will be crucial to Adorno's thinking about art. It is in engaging with a particular manifestation of a contradiction in society that one becomes aware of the need for thinking beyond that manifestation in the direction of the totality that produces the contradiction.

Another example from the Covid-19 pandemic can illustrate what Adorno means, and why Popper's piecemeal approach may not suffice to grasp the root of social pathologies. In Denmark, which farms millions of mink, it was discovered that they harboured a variant of the virus that might be immune to the vaccines being developed to counter it. This led to a moral dilemma, as a contemporary report makes clear (the cull went ahead, with distressing results):

If it turns out to be true that the mink variant would jeopardize our vaccines and that there's a strong chance that thousands or even millions of people will therefore die if we don't cull the minks, you could make the case that a cull is the lesser of two evils. But we just don't have enough data right now to know whether that's true.

We do, however, know one thing with certainty. The fact that we are being forced to choose between two reasonable impulses—wanting to prevent animal suffering and wanting to prevent human suffering—is the result of another decision made: to farm thousands and thousands of animals in close quarters and unsanitary conditions.

Rather than there being a morally secure, rational way of deciding between the two courses of action specific to the virus in the mink, relating the dilemma beyond itself to the functioning of mass animal farming for the fashion market shows that society itself is, in Adorno's terms, 'false'. It functions in a way which makes properly rational choices impossible. As long as this kind of production—which embodies what *DE* contended about modern rationalization's instrumental relationship to nature—continues there is no right way of dealing with what it produces.

Looked at in this way, Adorno's at first sight questionable idea that society is itself contradictory starts to make sense and suggests his prescience with respect to the effects of modern exploitation of nature. He contends that if a society is a collective entity for the self-preservation of its members, aspects of society which work against this—like cruel and pointless animal farming for profit—make the notion of 'society' senseless and irrational. Such choices between unacceptable alternatives are fundamental to the totality of contemporary capitalism, which creates situations where there is no good option. The climate crisis also makes this abundantly clear, and Adorno's approach is vindicated by the fact that only by looking beyond piecemeal forms of analysis and seeing things in terms of the totality has the seriousness of the contemporary situation of the world become fully apparent. This is not possible in the kind of terms proposed by Popper.

The totality is accessible, then, via the contradictions that become manifest in the attempt to interpret specific phenomena: 'The interpretation of the facts leads to the totality, without the latter itself being a fact' (GS 8 p. 292) of the kind traditional theory regards as the basis of justified cognition. It might appear that interpretation would then lead to a regress, where the contradictions involved in a moral choice are a result of the contradictions involved in factory farming, which are a result of the development of particular forms of commodification of nature, and so on. However, in line with his seeing philosophical theories as responses to historical tensions, Adorno points out that the demand for a theory of systemic social pressures beyond the control of the individuals who both undergo them and bring them about does not arise in the same way for pre-modern societies: 'It is...no coincidence that theory of society in an emphatic sense only arose with the industrial revolution and with emerging economic liberalism'.

Adorno repeatedly stresses that, in contrast to the success of the natural sciences, despite its 'advanced age, sociology does not show the least propensity to get closer to the ideal of a real theory of society'. In the terms of traditional theory, rejection of the idea that a theory of society should be critical in the way Adorno demands is linked to adherence to the fact–value distinction (you can't derive 'ought' from 'is'). The distinction is often seen as a logical one, and is part of what leads to the demand for value-freedom, facts being supposedly of a logically different status to values. However, Adorno points out that the distinction, like sociology itself, emerges in specifically modern social circumstances. Its emergence in the modern period is, he contends, part of the dialectic of Enlightenment, where increased factual knowledge and the resulting increase in control over nature became divorced from values that would mean they are employed for the good of society: 'in a phase in which means and ends are torn apart for the sake of the domination of nature...rationality of means progresses along with undiminished or even increasing irrationality of the ends' (GS 8 p. 560). He also points out, with respect to the distinction as it is often understood: 'If Popper concedes that the scientistic ideals of objectivity and value-freedom are for their part values, then that extends into the truth of judgements; their sense implies the "evaluating" idea that a true judgement is better than a false one' (GS 8 p. 346).

Truth and value

The idea of truth as a value, which at the time of the debate was not that widely held, has echoes in contemporary mainstream philosophy. Philosopher Huw Price argues that truth can be seen as a norm in human communication, and 'what matters is that speakers think that there is such a norm—that they take themselves to be governed by it—not that their view be somehow confirmed by science or metaphysics'. Philosopher Hilary Putnam contends that: 'judgments of coherence, simplicity and so on are presupposed by physical science. Yet coherence, simplicity and the like are values'. He therefore concludes: 'my pragmatist teachers were right: "knowledge of facts presupposes knowledge of values." But the history of the philosophy of science in the last half century has largely been a history of attempts...to evade this issue'. There is consequently a need for 'rethinking the whole dogma...that facts are objective and values are subjective and "never the twain shall meet"'. A pragmatist approach in analytical philosophy here coincides with Adorno's dialectical approach to questions of subject and object, and with his view of sociology as needing to develop theory in a manner which is precluded by the criteria of traditional theory.

Adorno derives part of his stance from Hegel's notion of 'immanent critique', 'the confrontation of the thing "*Sache*" with what it, of its own accord, according to its concept, claims to be'

(GS 8 p. 259), which is necessarily evaluative. In the present case this is 'the confrontation of what a society presents itself as and what it is' (GS 8 p. 347), rather than criticism based on a 'view from nowhere', which would rely on a dogmatic assertion of value from outside the particular social context. The liberal norm of free and fair exchange, for example, is 'universally developed', but 'becomes its own opposite' in late capitalism. Nobody can justifiably argue against the norm of free and fair exchange, and we cannot do without exchange as the 'measure of comparability', but exchange can become a means of oppression, as the creation of massive Third World debt by First World economic practices shows.

Discussion of society for Adorno is, then, inherently normative, because the concept of society itself only makes sense in normative terms. A society is not a random aggregate of people, and any society can come into conflict with its concept when it fails to fulfil normative demands inherent in that concept. Fundamental to Adorno's view, as we have seen, is the fact that we have the means to obviate many forms of human suffering, but that the organization of society so far fails to do this: 'if hunger is nevertheless present in a society in which hunger would be avoidable now and here, in view of the existing and obviously possible abundance of goods, then this demands the abolition of hunger through intervention in the relations of production' (GS 8 p. 347). There is no 'clash of values' here, because the idea that one could advocate values that condone other people starving makes no sense if one thinks a society is an organization for the self-preservation and development of its members. The madness here is reproduced on a global scale: 'Whilst the abundance of goods which could be produced everywhere and at the same time makes the battle for raw materials and markets ever more anachronistic, humankind is divided up into a few armed power blocks' (GS 3 p. 230). It is hard for us to imagine a state where such division would not pertain, but that is, for Adorno, not a reason to give up criticism of the status quo: 'The reification...has become so dense that every spontaneity, even the mere idea of the true facts of the matter, has necessarily become an extravagant utopia, an aberrant sectarianism' (GS 3 p. 231).

Hyperbolic as this assertion from 'Elements of Antisemitism' may be, when Adorno and Horkheimer wrote it in *DE* they were looking at societies which were annihilating millions of people for reasons which had nothing to do with what those people were and did. In the contemporary world, such an assertion also seems less extreme than it would have done even a few years ago. The questionable notion that we inhabit a 'post-truth' era—better would be an era of what Hannah Arendt called 'lying as a way of life'—adverts to the dangers in complex societies where accurate sources of information compete with massive disinformation of every kind in the new media. Almost anyone can be taken in by such disinformation, given the frequent lack of straightforward ways of identifying it, and the tendency to confirmation bias. Adorno's focus with regard to theories of society is particularly resonant now, in the face of the grotesque wealth inequalities in societies subjected to neoliberal economics, and the concomitant withdrawal from collective concern for the welfare of those societies' less fortunate members. What is perhaps most striking in these developments, and what makes Adorno still relevant to understanding them, is that many of those who suffer their worst consequences support the political forces which are the source of their suffering.

The social and the psychological

In *The Authoritarian Personality*, contemporary echoes abound: 'it is becoming increasingly plain that people very frequently do not behave in such a way as to further their material interests, even when it is clear to them what these interests are' (GS 9.1 p. 159). More important is often a person's 'larger group identification, as if his point of view were determined more by his need to support this group and to suppress opposite ones than by rational consideration of his own interests' (GS 9.1 p. 162). Many aspects of contemporary racism can be seen in such terms, and the reasons why relate to what Adorno says about fascism, namely that:

> in order to be successful as a political movement, it must have a mass basis....Since by its very nature it favors the few at the expense of the many, it cannot possibly demonstrate that it will so improve the situation of most people that their real interests will be served. It must therefore make its major appeal, not to rational self-interest, but to emotional needs—often to the most primitive and irrational wishes and fears. (GS 9.1 p. 162)

This leads to a further way in which projection plays a role in how the modern world is constituted: 'those who suffer from social pressure may frequently tend to transfer this pressure onto others rather than to join hands with their fellow victims' (GS 9.1 p. 275). But why is it that people aim their aggression at what are so often the wrong targets?

The difficulty here arises from assessing how the kind of explanation derived from psychoanalysis relates to explanation based on socio-economic structures. For Adorno, the super-ego provides a link between the two, but that raises questions in relation to what specific individuals do in real-world circumstances. He tends to see the individual as inherently a product of structural pressures, which means the ego is the object of the super-ego. But how is it that people are able to resist such pressures at all? Freud thought this involved strengthening the ego against the id, whereas Adorno sees the need to strengthen the ego against the super-ego: 'The only true force against the principle of Auschwitz would be autonomy, if I may use the Kantian expression; the force of reflection, or self-determination, of not going along with things' (GS 10.2 p. 679). However, this still does not fully explain what makes some people actually resist, despite all the social pressures of the context of delusion.

Historians tend to say that they cannot find a common psychological, social, or political denominator for those who resisted the Nazis in Germany. Adorno's reflections on freedom and the 'additional factor', the motivational impulse to act that eludes straightforward normative explanation we considered in Chapter 3, can play an explanatory role here, but it also suggests a further dialectic. If the individual has been co-opted into conformity with distorted social relations which license barbarism, extra-rational impulses that can motivate individual heroic moral action can also be the basis of appalling actions. A threshold between holding a conviction and actually acting in terms of it is in play in both. At the same time, many of the perpetrators were indeed in certain respects just a product of those particular objective historical and social circumstances. Such people often went on to live 'respectable' lives after the war when social conditions radically changed. Adorno's insistence on the primacy of the totality helps here: in the objective circumstances of a peaceful, increasingly prosperous post-war Germany, the impetus to transfer social pressure is reduced, though it does not, of course, disappear. At the same time, Adorno's focus on the 'primacy of the objective' arguably does not always adequately explain how, despite all the objective factors that constitute the subject, some subjects still can manage to act in terms of the autonomy he sees as necessary for the avoidance of a repetition of Auschwitz (Figure 6).

One of Adorno's most insightful accounts of how social pressure functions is, perhaps surprisingly, to be found in his research on the popularity of an astrology column in a Los Angeles newspaper. This exemplifies his conviction that attention to 'the experience of the particular' can be the key to grasping social phenomena. His assumptions about the nature of modern social relations are summed up in this analysis of how contexts of delusion function:

Thus people even of supposedly 'normal' mind are prepared to accept systems of delusions for the simple reason that it is too

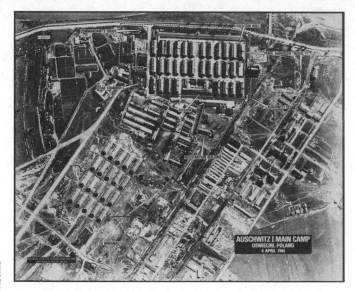

6. Auschwitz I Main Camp.

difficult indeed to distinguish such systems from the equally
inexorable and equally opaque one under which they actually
have to live out their lives. This is pretty well reflected by astrology.
(GS 9.2 p. 110)

Such delusion is echoed in the contemporary world by the
widespread adherence to conspiracy theories as explanations of
what is going wrong, even though the information that would
allow people to understand the real economic and political causes
of social and political ills is in certain respects more readily
available than ever before. The Covid pandemic once again
provides plenty of examples, notably the theories that the
pandemic is not real, or is massively exaggerated, and is part of a
plan of 'those in power' to gain more control over the population.
Such theories clearly have their roots in people's sense that what is
happening is happening 'above their heads', and their

accompanying aggressive claims to superior insight in advancing such theories are based on a deep sense of insecurity: 'What somebody has as an opinion becomes, as their possession, a component of their person, and what invalidates the opinion is registered by the unconscious and pre-conscious as if they themselves were being damaged' (GS 10.2 p. 576), so they defend it even more stubbornly.

The reasons Adorno has again become a focus of attention in a world threatened by fascism and climate change are very apparent in the following: 'it seems that in eras of decline of social systems, with the insecurity and anxiety widespread in such eras, paranoid tendencies in people are evinced and often channelized by institutions wishing to distract such tendencies from their objective reasons' (GS 10.2 pp. 119–20). Paranoia is in one sense the result of another dialectic of Enlightenment: 'Irrationality is not necessarily a force operating outside the range of rationality: it may result from the processes of rational self-preservation "run amuck"' (GS 10.2 p. 15). People rightly sense that things are working against them, but oppose this in politically deluded ways, which often involve projection. In the face of the Trump administration's irrevocable tearing apart of hundreds of immigrant families—in the name of the idea that immigrants are 'stealing American jobs', many of which had been outsourced to countries with very low labour costs by US corporations—the following has particular resonance: 'So-called national renewal movements in an era in which nationalism is obsolete are particularly susceptible to sadistic practices' (GS 10.2 p. 690). Such nationalism 'is as evil as it is because in the era of international communication and of supra-national blocs it cannot really believe in itself, and has to exaggerate itself to a boundless extent in order to persuade itself and others that it still really has any substance' (GS 10.2 p. 689).

Adorno suggests another dimension of the distorting effects of such lack of substance when discussing projection on the part of the Nazi anti-Semite: 'It is as if the anti-Semite could not sleep quietly until he has transformed the whole world into the very same paranoid system by which he is beset' (GS 9.1 p. 303). In consequence 'the idea of eternal Jewish guilt can be understood as a projection of the prejudiced person's own repressed guilt feelings', and this means that 'The disproportion between the guilt and the punishment induces him, rather, to pursue his hatred beyond any limits and thus to prove to himself and to others that he must be right' (GS 9.1 p. 304). This illustrates the tendency of subjectivity to function in terms of domination that we encountered in earlier chapters, and the question is how this kind of narcissistic perversion of self-assertion can be countered.

In the face of the crushing evidence of the way social delusion has functioned in 20th-century politics, and continues to function in the 21st century, it would be naive to expect Adorno to offer generalized answers as to how delusions can be overcome. How can one affect the psychological make-up of individuals who have, like the Nazi anti-Semite, been influenced by objective, systemic pressures, without first changing the systems that lead to those pressures? Adorno sees the basic dialectic here as follows: 'Society is a total process in which people are enveloped, steered, and formed by objectivity, yet on the other hand have effects on it; psychology can as little be merged into sociology as the individual can be into its biological species and its natural history' (GS 8 p. 563). The same characterological traits may, for example, be pernicious in one social context, and beneficial in another, and the preponderance of objective factors of various kinds will affect which is the case.

In 'Education after Auschwitz' Adorno sees the problem in anthropological terms. The necessity of self-preservation means 'coldness . . . is a basic feature . . . of the constitution of human beings' (GS 10.2 p. 687), so that the capacity for identification with other people is, when it comes to the crunch, subordinated to self-interest. He argues that society has 'for millennia' been based on the pursuit of self-interest. Clearly, from the very beginning of human existence, survival with minimal technological means of self-defence entails such self-interest, which is a result of objective pressure. At the same time, however, there have to be some means of accounting for the development of cooperation, non-repressive sociality, altruism, etc. Adorno does not in any way dispute their existence, but it is hard to reconcile it with an anthropological account based mainly on self-preservation. Adorno touches on this in a discussion of Kant on practical reason: 'but that reason which makes itself independent and directs itself towards truth is, so to speak, a dialectical product, so to speak the child of that self-preserving, in the normal sense, practical reason'. *Why* that non-instrumental product of instrumental reason emerges at all remains unclear. It can be argued that this is actually more of an empirical question for historical anthropology than a philosophical issue concerning 'basic features of the constitution of human beings'.

Not all forms of non-repressive sociality are explicable in terms of self-interest. Accounting for what can prevent the 'war of all against all' lies at the heart of political philosophy. If reason is exclusively 'instrumental'—what Weber terms 'zweckrational', rational in terms of ends to be achieved by whatever are the most effective means—certain dimensions of human life become hard to explain, and the idea of political progress can seem doomed. Adorno's pupil Jürgen Habermas sees the problem in Adorno's position as deriving from a too restrictive conception of rationality. For Habermas, rationality is not always explicable in terms of instrumental self-preservation, because it entails communication. It is implausible to see all communication in terms of the exercise of power over the other, because we can, for example, acknowledge that the other is right and we are wrong, by appreciating what Habermas terms the 'forceless force of the better argument'. As Huw Price suggests, communication only makes sense at all on the basis of adherence to shared norms. Habermas's exploration of such norms in what he terms 'communicative action' opens up dimensions of social analysis that are sometimes missing in Adorno, for example with respect to the law, or to what can make everyday social life function relatively successfully. The fact is that Adorno does not, in the main, focus on issues concerning language and philosophy in the kind of terms suggested by Habermas. His approach to how alternatives to instrumental reason can be conceived is developed mainly in relation to the understanding of the arts.

Chapter 7
Art and philosophy

Universal and particular

Adorno's never-completed *Aesthetic Theory* (first published 1970) was to have had this fragment by the early German Romantic theorist Friedrich Schlegel as its motto: 'In what one calls philosophy of art, one of the two is usually missing; either philosophy or art'. The challenge is, then, to find a form of philosophy which illuminates art without obscuring what art 'says' that philosophy is unable to say. The opening of the book suggests the radicality of Adorno's approach: 'It has become taken for granted that nothing concerning art is to be taken for granted any more, neither in art nor in its relation to the whole, not even its right to exist' (GS 7 p. 9). We have seen how Adorno links pathologies in modern societies to the culture industry, which reinforces the status quo and undermines autonomous critical judgement. We also saw in his questionable response to jazz how his analysis could become inadequate in relation to the detail of the phenomena he is criticizing. The tension between these two aspects of his critiques of cultural phenomena recurs in Adorno's reflections on art and aesthetics.

Art depends on making particular aspects of the world meaningful in new ways; philosophy, on the other hand, can often be seen in the terms suggested by American philosopher Wilfrid Sellars:

'The aim of philosophy, abstractly formulated, is to understand how things in the broadest possible sense of the term hang together in the broadest possible sense of the term'. The question is how particularity and universality in art and in philosophy relate, and what this tells us about each. Reflecting on art and Nazism in an essay written in 1945, Adorno states:

> Since philosophy in the broadest sense, the general consciousness of the people, has been brought more and more under the sway of science and technical civilization, the relationship between art and truth has been profoundly affected. There is no longer any unifying common focus between knowledge or science on the one hand and art on the other, as there is no common focus between science and philosophy or religion. (GS 20.2 p. 418)

Referring to Kant and Hegel in *Aesthetic Theory*, Adorno claims: 'The great philosophical aesthetics were concordant with art to the extent that they conceptualised what was evidently universal in it; in accordance with a stage of mind [*Geist*] in which philosophy and others of its forms, like art, were not yet torn apart' (GS 7 pp. 495–6). Art in the period of Kant and German Idealism can be seen as reconciling particular and universal: Beethoven's appeals in the Ninth Symphony to the brotherhood of humankind are realized in very individual music that has shown itself to have enduring universal significance. Adorno draws parallels between Beethoven's integration of individual kinds of new musical material into established forms, like the sonata, and Hegel's integration of things that initially appear contradictory into his dialectical system, where the 'whole is the true'. For Adorno, as we saw, Hegel's assumption that there can be a rational integration of individual and society comes up against the brutality of modern capitalism. In this situation art's integration of diverse and conflicting material via its formal organization in 'judgementless synthesis', rather than through concepts, can no longer be taken for granted. The unified aesthetic whole is now 'untrue' because it simulates something that is missing in reality.

In consequence 'What has been called the "idea" of arts during the age of great speculative philosophy has come to be regarded as an obsolescent metaphysical prejudice' (GS 20.2 p. 418).

Modernist art undoubtedly does involve the breakdown and rejection of established ways of integrating material into a whole. This is apparent, for example, in the abandonment of tonality and the search for new ordering principles by Schoenberg and others, in the move away from representational forms of painting, and perhaps most famously in Marcel Duchamp's 'ready-made' sculpture, *Fountain*, which involved signing a urinal and putting it in an art exhibition. Establishing what implications the breakdown of received forms has for metaphysics is, however, not straightforward. Metaphysics has traditionally been linked to questions about the meaning of existence. Adorno asserts, though, as we saw, that 'Already before Auschwitz it was an affirmative lie in the face of historical experiences to attribute any positive sense to existence. That has consequences right into the form of works of art' (GS 7 p. 229). He does not, then, endorse approaches that regard art as a means of overcoming human existence's lack of metaphysical meaning. So what kind of sense can art make, once it cannot rely on established forms, and is untied from any kind of positive metaphysical meaning?

Adorno talks of 'the aesthetic impossibility of a reestablishment of an order of art just from the will to such an order, without this order being substantially present to us any more in the thing itself and in the world in which we live'. The order found in the art of a period cannot, therefore, just be imposed by an individual artist independently of the social order. This might sound implausible, in that a modern artist who wishes to paint beautiful landscapes as a relief from the ugliness of everyday life may be perfectly able to do this, if they have the requisite skill and talent. For Adorno, though, this would not establish an 'order of art' that was an adequate response to the modern world. He is not denying the possibility of the painter doing what they want, or of people finding it aesthetically pleasing, but he is denying that the resulting paintings are 'true' of the world in which they are located.

Referring to music in the essay from 1945, Adorno sums up the position of those who reject the radical music of Schoenberg and others:

> The world has become so ugly and terrifying, so runs the argument, that art should no longer dwell upon distorted forms, discords and everything branded as being destructive, but should return to the realm of beauty and harmony. The world of destruction, terror and sadism is the world of Hitler. And art should show its opposition to it by going back to its traditional ideals. (GS 20.2 p. 422)

His position is the polar opposite of this: for him the avant-garde's 'supposed spirit of negativism and destruction' is what 'kept faith to Beethoven's humanism by expressing in an undiluted way the sufferings, the anguish, the fear, under which we live today long before the political crisis arose, instead of covering it up by idle comfort. It thus has maintained the link between music and philosophical truth' (GS 20.2 p. 422). Art and philosophy are analogous in their concern with how societies order themselves and the world. Just as successful science depends to a great extent on disinterested enquiry, rather than being wholly led by extraneous purposes, art succeeds for Adorno where aesthetic challenges are confronted, with no intended social effect getting in the way. Why the aesthetic challenges faced by the serious artist involve 'the relationship between essential philosophical truth and art' is, though, not explained by what he says in this context.

The order of art

In lectures on Aesthetics, Adorno tells his students: 'you should from the outset free yourself from that concept of philosophy...which is supposed to consist of epistemology and aesthetics...as a kind of special science, and arrive at the position of seeing philosophy really as the self-consciousness of the epoch'. Art can equally be seen as 'the self-consciousness of the epoch', and the question is how art's forms of self-consciousness—its critical reflection on human relationships to the world—relate to those of philosophy. Adorno claims that 'The greatness of Beethoven has to be understood in musical concepts first. Yet, the fact that he was bound up with humanistic philosophy permeates his whole work and determines even the most subtle details of his musicianship' (GS 20.2 p. 434). So how does philosophy permeate the musical work and other forms of art?

One way of answering this is apparent in the following, where Beethoven again plays a decisive role. In contrast to the nature of music in cultures bound more by tradition, modern Western 'classical' music from Monteverdi to the present keeps changing, often in very radical ways. No serious composer would now compose in the manner of Mozart, even though it is perfectly possible to do so. Composers continually question prevailing norms, and this is echoed in philosophy. The questioning takes place to the point where the most demanding music, particularly from Beethoven onwards—his 'Great Fugue' for String Quartet Op. 133 still challenges many listeners even today—risks no longer having an audience. In this context the idea that what happens in music is linked to other tendencies in modernity makes more sense. If, as Marx put it, 'All that's solid melts into air', when capitalism replaces traditional feudal forms of order, art's very mutability can be linked to the disintegration of such forms of order in other spheres. Beethoven is located between the heroic individualism that is enabled by the early stages of capitalism and is reflected, for example, in the Fifth Symphony, and, in his later work, especially in the late string quartets, a questioning of received musical forms because they may no longer convey anything universal.

The music following Beethoven can be seen in such a perspective as relating to the disintegration of the German Idealist attempt to construct a unified system that could overcome the antagonisms generated by modernity. Ever more triumphant symphonic conclusions in Bruckner and other late Romantics involve a sense that such musical triumph is achieved despite what is happening in the real world. Adorno claims that, with Mahler, music 'caught up in an original manner with Nietzsche's insight that the system and its unbroken unity, the semblance/illusion [*Schein*] of reconciliation was not honest' (GS 13 p. 213). The differing conclusions of Mahler's symphonies, from triumphant reconciliation in the Second to slow extinction in the Ninth, convey the growing sense of unease in European culture that precedes the world wars. Modern art, then, becomes perennially controversial, because a real reconciliation of individual freedom and social order is not achieved. In these terms, the choice is between art either creating the questionable appearance of such order or responding to the lack of reconciliation which underlies the historical developments.

Thomas Mann's novel *Doktor Faustus* (1947), about a fictional 20th-century German composer obsessed with coming up with a new, strict form of modern musical order, for which Adorno advised Mann on questions of composition, explores these issues. On the one hand, new forms of order become the aim of serious art, and Mann's novel connects the problem of order in music with that of social and political order; on the other, there is no consensus about the value of such forms. Mann's composer at one point asserts that 'even a ridiculous order is still better than none at all', suggesting the anxiety that accompanies this issue, and the violent ways in which those like the Nazis imposed social order. Adorno is a thoroughgoing modernist in these questions, because he sees no way of going back to traditional forms of social and aesthetic order: 'The thought of future renewal, whether it be in great and rounded works of art, or in the happy consonance of music and society, just denies what happened and what can be suppressed but cannot be made not to have happened' (GS 12 p. 36). For him the pursuit of new forms may keep open a sense of possible liberation: 'In the liberation of form which all genuine art desires, the liberation of society is encoded above all else, because form, the aesthetic connection of everything individual, represents the social relationship in the work of art' (GS 7 p. 379). How, though, does what happens to form in works of art relate to liberation in society?

Art, society, and politics

Debates in Europe over art and aesthetics, particularly from the second half of the 19th century onwards, and particularly in left-wing circles, often revolve around a perceived clash between 'formalism', for which the form of art is most essential to what makes it art, and criticism of concentration on formal matters in the name of art's social, emotional, political, etc. 'content', and its potential for promoting social transformation. Taking up ideas from the playwright and poet Bertolt Brecht, Walter Benjamin talked of the 'politicisation of aesthetics' as a means of opposing the fascist 'aestheticisation of politics', evident in choreographed mass rallies, etc. Adorno is, though, more circumspect: 'All attempts to give back to art what it doubts by giving it a social function…have failed' (GS 7 p. 9). He insists instead on art's 'autonomy', without which it loses its connection to freedom by being subordinated to social purposes that are extraneous to the formal demands it involves. At the same time, he contends that art is inseparable from the social and political circumstances in which it is located. He seeks to mediate the clash between formalism and political engagement by the dialectical claim that 'The campaign against formalism'—in the Soviet Union and other communist countries—'ignores the fact that the form to which the content is subjected is itself sedimented content' (GS 7 p. 218). The notion of form as 'sedimented content' is the core of Adorno's thinking about art, and can explain why he links form in art to questions of freedom.

Both in metaphysics and in aesthetics, 'form' is often thought of in relation to 'matter', and the question is what 'matter' is in works of art. In sculpture, for example, it would seem obvious that it is the stone, clay, or whatever, given shape by the sculptor, but that is precisely not Adorno's point. He generally refers to 'material', rather than 'matter', and uses the term in relation to all the arts, especially music. The material in question, in the form of existing artistic techniques, makes demands on the artist, which 'derive...from the fact that the "material" is itself sedimented spirit, something social, which has been preformed by the consciousness of people. As former subjectivity which has forgotten itself this objective spirit of the material has its own laws of motion' (GS 12 p. 39). The material is, then, another manifestation of 'second nature', produced by subjects, which exerts objective pressure on the artist, even when they are not fully aware of it. It does so in ways related to manifestations of humanly produced second nature such as economic and ideological pressures that we encountered in earlier chapters, and this is why modern art raises questions about freedom.

For the sculptor what they form is, then, not just the material in question, but also the history of what sculptors have done with it, and how this was received in society. The same applies to the other arts. Notes in music consist just of sound waves that occur elsewhere in nature. They become 'material' in Adorno's sense when they are ordered into a harmonic system, and into the ways the system is employed in differing historical and musical contexts, where what was objectively wrong at one time can become right at another. The artist who engages seriously with art has to resist the objective pressure of existing forms and practices:

> Instead of being a decisive means to express fundamentals about human existence and human society, art has assumed the function of a realm of consumer goods among others, measured only according to what people 'can get out of it', the amount of gratification or pleasure it provides them with or, to a certain extent, its historical or educational value. (GS 20.2 p. 418)

Art and philosophy are both subject to the pressure of second nature, and they try to distance themselves from society by seeking autonomy, but 'no authentic work of art, and no true philosophy ever has…exhausted itself in itself, in its being-in-itself. They always stood in relation to the real life-process of the society from which they separated themselves'. This separation means they point to 'a state in which freedom was realised' (GS 10.1 p. 16).

This dialectical combination of distance from and relationship to society can make Adorno's conception hard to grasp. The distance in question is dependent on continual critical reflection, based on the likelihood of any received cultural form involving the perpetuation of delusion. However, the 'Gnostic' tendency we observed with respect to Adorno's critique of jazz and the culture industry can lead him to questionable generalizations about the social reception of art. In a *Spiegel* interview, Adorno, having claimed Mozart's *The Marriage of Figaro* is 'no longer Figaro' if shown on TV, is asked: 'Are you, then, of the opinion that music on TV is for now meaningless ritual [*Brimborium*]?', to which he replies, 'Yes, that is my opinion. TV concerts and TV operas are a piece of empty cultural activity' (GS 19 p. 569). He elsewhere says much the same thing about symphonies on the radio. Adorno seems to have no concern with how very many people gain their access to great music. I developed a lifelong interest in conductor Wilhelm Furtwängler after hearing one of his recordings of Beethoven's Ninth Symphony on a transistor radio: even the poor reproduction could not hide that something extraordinary was happening in the music.

The historical pressure that helps account for Adorno's 'Gnostic' position is clear when he asserts in 1945: 'Only those who know to what extent artistic and especially musical questions are involved with political issues throughout German cultural life can fully understand the emotional role played by the hatred against the music of the avantgarde within all reactionary and repressive groups of German society' (GS 20.2 p. 436). Expression of 'fundamentals about human existence and human society' depends to a great extent on social and historical context, and the immediate post-war German historical context makes Adorno's partisanship for the avant-garde as the only real manifestation of freedom understandable. At the same time, he tends to see music predominantly in terms of the specific philosophico-historical picture we have been tracing. In other contexts it becomes clear that too much that matters about music can thereby be neglected.

Expression and system

The consolation provided by music when someone is faced with experiences of loss and grief no doubt has historical and ideological components that can be reflected on in Adorno's manner, and the music in question may have been co-opted by the culture industry. However, the immediacy of the consoling or uplifting aesthetic experience, which can offer a temporary form of liberation, need not be erased by such factors. It seems mistaken to undervalue that experience in the name of exclusive focus on philosophical understanding of its relationship to the socio-historical totality: existential dimensions of art are not always reducible to socio-historical ones. Daniel Barenboim observes of music that it is 'so clearly able to teach you so many things', and can also 'serve as a means of escape from precisely those things'. Historical examples are legion where the practice of music and art of all kinds enabled people to sustain hope in what were objectively hopeless circumstances. Adorno takes too little account of such phenomena, despite his persistent concern with how art may convey hope.

Such existential responses to music do, however, make more sense in terms of Adorno's reflections on mimesis and expression in art. There is a tension in art between expression, and the artistic means via which it is realized: 'As something expressive music behaves mimetically, imitating in the way gestures respond to a stimulus' (GS 13 p. 170). Elsewhere he puts it like this: 'In music it is not a question of meaning but of gestures. To the extent to which it is language it is, like notation in its history, a language sedimented from gestures' (GS 18 p. 154). Immediate responses in the form of gestures are part of natural, embodied human existence, hence their connection to the emotional significance of music as a non-verbal form of expression. The 'sedimented' form of the expression of these responses is, though, located in the intersubjective, social realm, for instance in the collective development of objective rules for the notation of music. Consequently: 'This mimetic moment gradually coalesces in music with the rational moment, the mastery of the material; how both work on each other is music's history' (GS 18 p. 154). The technical resource of notation enables a massive expansion of musical form, because it counters the limitations of memory, and offers possibilities for the development of expressive complexity. At the same time, notation can rigidify music into a series of rule-bound conventions. Musicians have to transcend these in performance if something aesthetically significant is to result—hence the connection to freedom—and such transcendence, in turn, requires the mimetic.

Adorno describes the fundamental contradiction that structures large parts of his writings on the Western classical music tradition as follows:

> The music which we still directly inhabit—and it begins precisely with Bach—labours from the beginning with an internal difficulty, a contradiction. On the one hand, it is enclosed in a system, the system of triads, of keys, and their relationships. On the other, the subject seeks to express itself in it, wants, instead of every norm that is just externally imposed, to produce lawfulness from out of itself. (GS 18 p. 435)

This links music to the dialectical reflections on subject and object we have encountered in earlier chapters. The social subject produces the 'second nature' of tonality—Adorno insists that tonality is not based on 'natural' intervals because these are now mathematically rationalized in the tempered scale, which, from Bach onwards, expands formal possibilities in music. Tonality's restrictions on permissible dissonance then come to be seen as inhibiting the subject, and this leads the subject to seek ways of freeing itself from the second nature which it at the same time reproduces. Beethoven plays a decisive role in the move to the new situation, which is explored in *Philosophy of New Music*. Adorno argues that Beethoven is sometimes able successfully to negotiate the relationship between individual expression and the existing objective constraints of musical form. The 'setting' of Beethoven's music is 'socially transmitted forms'—like sonata, variation, rondo, etc.: as such, it is 'ascetic with respect to the private expression of feelings'. His music also reflects the social conflicts of its day, and yet at the same time 'draws the fullness and power of the individual from this asceticism' (GS 4 p. 170), in the kind of reconciliation of individual and social which Hegel seeks in his philosophical account of rationality in modern society.

Adorno's most extreme position results from his interpretation of the social and philosophical significance of the 'new music' of the Second Viennese School, which parts company with 'traditional music'. The latter

> had to make do with a very limited number of combinations of notes, especially in the vertical [i.e. in terms of harmony]. It had to get used to always achieving the specific once again through constellations of the universal, which, paradoxically, saw the universal as identical with the unique. Beethoven's whole oeuvre is the explication of this paradox. (GS 12 p. 55)

This reconciliation of universal and particular, in which the individual composer exercises their freedom by manipulating the possibilities of pre-given musical material, gives way to a radical new situation, via the loosening of forms and extension of permissible dissonance.

The vital transitional figure here is Richard Wagner, whom Adorno links to the dissolution of the kind of philosophical system advanced by Hegel: 'In art no less than philosophy the systems aim to produce the synthesis of the manifold from out of themselves....With Wagner this is no longer the case' (GS 13 pp. 46–7). Before Wagner, 'In Beethoven and right into high romanticism the harmonic expressive values are fixed: dissonance stands for the negative, consonance for the positive and fulfilment' (GS 13. p. 64). This stability dissolves with Wagner's use of chromaticism, which opens up more complex, ambiguous forms of expression, at the same time as posing new questions about how to organize musical material. The fact that anti-systematic philosophers Schopenhauer and Nietzsche play a substantive historical role in any attempt to understand Wagner's music justifies Adorno's link of music and philosophy in this case, but things get more difficult with respect to music and art after Wagner.

The dilemma that results for new music is seen by Adorno as follows: 'Since the compositional process is measured only by the particular form of each work, not by tacitly accepted universal demands, what is good or bad music can no longer be "learned"' (GS 12 p. 18). In principle, any combination of notes is allowed, once restrictions on dissonance based on tonality are no longer binding. However, in reality: 'The dissolution of everything pre-given has not resulted in the possibility of manipulating every material and technique at one's own discretion' (GS 12 p. 25). Whereas degrees of dissonance and consonance in traditional music are a pre-given basis for the build-up and release of tension which enables formal coherence, the 'emancipation of dissonance' means this way of creating form can no longer function. Schoenberg himself suggests a key difficulty of atonality when he talks of only becoming able to use it 'to construct larger forms by following a text or poem', the lack of tonal resolutions having ruled out a central way of structuring a larger composition. This leads him to the idea of 'composition with 12 tones', where each note of the chromatic scale is used to construct a 12-note 'row', which then is used to determine the pattern of notes in the whole composition. For Adorno, in tonal music: 'The harmony of particular and universal corresponded to the classical-liberal model of society. As in that model the totality asserted itself behind the scenes as the invisible hand, by dint of the individual spontaneities and over their heads' (GS 17 p. 284). What results from the breakdown of this link between tonality and social order is music whose truth 'seems rather to be contained in the fact that it denies the meaning of organised society, of which it wishes to know nothing, by organised emptiness of meaning, rather than being capable of producing meaning of its own accord. In the present conditions it is limited to determinate negation' (GS 12 p. 28). The music is, then, limited to the refusal to follow the direction given by the musical tradition, while yet depending on it as what it has to leave behind to make any sense at all.

'Philosophical music'

At this point Adorno's 'Gnostic' tendency re-emerges because of the way in which he analogizes music to philosophy: in doing so, he tends to exclude too many aspects of music's social significance by assimilating them to the meanings of 'organised society'. His interpretation of the frequent rejection of the new music of Schoenberg and others by the public is consequently too undifferentiated: 'The dissonances that scare them speak of their own condition: for this reason alone they are unbearable to them' (GS 12 p. 18). Audiences will, though, actually often accept dissonant modern music if the context in which it is presented makes sense to them, for example in a film. This can then lead to its acceptance in the concert hall, as can effective musical education. Moreover, children often have no difficulty with new music that adults may reject.

Adorno at times thinks too much in terms of what one might call 'philosophical music', that is the music that most obviously chimes with his philosophical concerns. In consequence, he overestimates—important as it undoubtedly is—the Second Viennese School's approach to composition, and tends towards what pianist and musicologist Charles Rosen has called an 'ethnocentric' stance, aspects of which we saw in his misjudgement of the significance of jazz. He makes similar reductive judgements with respect to Stravinsky, talking, for example, of the 'liquidation of the individual which Stravinsky's music celebrates' (GS 12 p. 174), and seeing him as a 'restoration of the past', rather than, like Schoenberg, as a progressive modernist. The contortions Adorno goes through to pass such negative judgements on pieces like the *Sacre du printemps* now just sound tendentious: 'Stravinsky sets out schemata of human forms of reaction which then became universal under the unavoidable pressure of late industrial society' (GS 12 p. 156), and his music is just 'music about music' (GS 12 p. 167). Stravinsky is not without his problematic aspects, especially in his neo-classical works, some of which arguably are just 'music about music', but the continuing importance of his best work testifies against Adorno's reductive judgements on him. Adorno claims with respect to new music of the Second Viennese School, in contrast, that 'only in the extremes is the essence of this music made clear; they alone permit the recognition of its truth-content' (GS 12 p. 13). Music has to live up to the most advanced 'state of the material' evident in the extremes of free atonality and dodecaphonic music. These testify to the situation in which 'universal and particular cannot be brought together again by an act of will; nor is tonality, as it was thought from time to time, restorable' (GS 17 p. 283). The simple objection to this is, though, that tonality does not need restoring: its possibilities are still being productively explored in all kinds of music.

In a characteristic move, Adorno applies his conception of the domination of nature to the understanding of new techniques in art, and proposes the following not very convincing dialectical reversal: 'The opposition of works of art against domination is mimesis of domination. They have to become like dominating behaviour, in order to produce something that is qualitatively different from the world of domination' (GS 7 p. 430). Nature, in the sense of that which is oppressed and repressed, is supposed to speak via what is opposed to it, that is technical command—'domination'—of complex musical material. What sounds in many ways furthest from nature, because its mimetic moment has been repressed in the gaining of technical command, is supposed to express what has been repressed in our relationship to internal and external nature. Schoenberg's *Erwartung*, which tracks, in highly organized but dissonant and expressive atonal music, the traumatic experience of a woman finding the body of her lover at night in a wood, exemplifies what Adorno intends. There is, though, no necessity to assume that only technically advanced music that fits Adorno's criteria can enable what is repressed to speak. His dialectical reversal is too dependent on a philosophical idea. This becomes apparent in the subsequent development of music. While atonality and dodecaphony still play a role in contemporary new music, they are largely seen as just one musical tool, rather than being mandatory.

The diversity of contemporary music is simply at odds with Adorno's philosophical appropriation of music. Who would now trust themself to make a general judgement on the 'state of the material' that would determine critical assessment of a piece of music's significance? Within many modern musical traditions the demand not just to repeat the past is widely accepted, but there is no one 'state of the material' which can be used to judge what is aesthetically significant and what isn't. The story of European music from Bach to Schoenberg and beyond that Adorno tells, and its connection to philosophy from Kant to Nietzsche, contains many revealing insights, but also leads to dead-ends and neglects too many other kinds of music. Where would music go next, if 'organised emptiness of meaning' is now the only expression of musical truth? That Adorno saw music at the end of the war in such terms is understandable, but his stance leaves too little room for assessing the diverse ways in which music continues to develop in differing social and political contexts.

Adorno's position on the denial of meaning in modernist art does, at the same time, point to something significant. There are reasons to question 'affirmative art' that ignores the persistence of a manifestly unjust world. His aesthetic reflections are sometimes more convincing when he explores the disintegration of redemptive metaphysics that would seek to make sense of the traumatic history of modernity. This exploration leaves more space for the articulation of other kinds of sense that still inform people's lives, despite the disintegration of metaphysical sense that would make history as a whole meaningful. By taking seriously the concrete failure of such metaphysics, new ways of making sense are opened up:

> The key to contemporary anti-art, with Beckett as its pinnacle, may be the idea of concretising that negation of sense; to discern something aesthetically meaningful in the relentless negation of metaphysical sense. The aesthetic principle of form is in itself, by synthesis of what is formed, the positing of sense, even where sense is repudiated by content. (GS 7 p. 403)

Even art which does acknowledge the destruction of meaning in its 'content'—for example, in Beckett's *Endgame*: 'Hamm: We're not beginning...to...to...mean something? Clov: Mean something? You and I mean something? (Short laugh)'—remains a resource for making sense. Such expressions of meaninglessness in artistic form constitute their own particular kind of meaning, which in Beckett is often bleakly comic.

Adorno, however, does not sufficiently attend to the everyday ways in which, as Albrecht Wellmer puts it, one still has to 'grant to art a *function in connection with* forms of non-aesthetic communication, or with a real change of relationships between self and world'. Significant art need not just be, as it largely is for Adorno, the 'presence in the forms of semblance of a state which does not yet exist'. There is a quasi-theological, utopian aspect to Adorno's 'Gnostic' insistence on true modern art's radical negation of meaning. Art is sometimes seen as mere semblance, so that only a total transformation of the world would be 'real'. The myriad ways in which art still actively intervenes in transforming the everyday world for the better can be neglected in such a perspective. Involvement with art as a social *practice* produces real changes in people's lives: art does not just offer a semblance of a utopian new world. The latter need not be excluded from thinking about art, but nor should the former (Figure 7).

Adorno was arguably better at writing about music he clearly liked, than about music he saw as philosophically important, let alone music he evidently disliked. His 'Gnostic' stance is, for example, less decisive in relation to music such as that of Gustav Mahler. In his writings on Mahler, Adorno achieves a kind of 'musical philosophy' by the way in which he engages with Mahler's compositions, mixing technical analysis with evocative descriptive passages that make one hear the music in new ways. He makes great sense, for example, of Mahler's use of hackneyed musical material:

> Every Mahler symphony asks how a living totality can emerge out of the ruins of the musical world of things. Mahler's music is not great despite the kitsch towards which it tends, but because its construction unties the tongue of kitsch, releasing the longing, which commerce just exploits, that is served by kitsch. (GS 13 p. 189)

The way that music which has been rendered meaningless—thing-like—by becoming a commodity makes new sense in Mahler's work is here conveyed by prose which reveals what cannot be described by objectifying musical analysis or by philosophical analogy.

Remarks like the following bring out the best in Adorno's focus on the working out of contradictions in his exploration of modern culture: 'in terms of the philosophy of history, Mahler's form approaches that of the novel. The musical material is pedestrian,

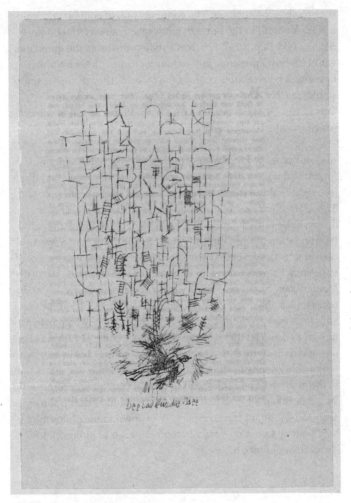

7. Paul Klee, *Death for the Idea*.

the presentation sublime. The configuration of content and style was no different in the novel of all novels, Flaubert's *Madame Bovary*' (GS 13 p. 209). Flaubert's style transforms the mundane world his novel presents, just as Mahler's music lives from the opposition between the 'course of the world', the repressive, unjust status quo that is manifest in banal musical material, and 'breakthrough', the evocation of a new, fulfilling world by music which transforms the banality.

Adorno's most productive approaches to art give full weight to formal issues, as well as to their historical significance, but he can lose sight of the aesthetic by assimilating it to the philosophical. This is what, for example, vitiates parts of *Philosophy of New Music*, as he himself later realized: 'The decisive thing, the interpretation of the compositions of Schoenberg, was always inadequate. In consequence it appeared that music was supposed to be completely dissolved into cognition' (GS 18 p. 165). In the Mahler book, and many smaller pieces on music, literature, and other topics, the interplay between philosophical interpretation and the evocation of the experience of art of those who participate in it offers a model that can counterbalance some of Adorno's one-sided theoretical approaches. The precarious balance between art and philosophy in Adorno's work is a reflection of the fact that in the modern period the status of *both* art and philosophy can no longer be taken for granted. At his best, though, Adorno shows, against a dominant trend, especially in anglophone philosophy, how art may sometimes offer better responses to philosophical issues than philosophy itself.

Chapter 8
Doing justice to things

The continuing importance of the idea of a 'dialectic of Enlightenment' was suggested by a recent internet meme: 'Do y'all remember, before the internet, that people thought the cause of stupidity was the lack of access to information? Yeah. It wasn't that'. As crisis piles on crisis in the countries, particularly in the Western world, that most emphatically espoused neoliberal economic and social policies, people's attempts to make sense of what is happening are more and more prone to delusion, even as the availability of information that could counter delusion increases. This might be seen as evident, for example, in the growing incidence of baseless conspiracy theories, and in the adoption of far-right politics, based on racist scapegoating, to account for systemic socio-economic problems, in a manner often reminiscent of the 1930s.

Adorno's suspicion of 'information' was already apparent in the 1931 Kierkegaard book, where he talks of the 'replacement of spontaneous thought by automatised conformity, that occurs in connection with modern forms of information' (GS 2 p. 230). The proliferation of information via the web often does not lead to a development of new ways of dealing with political and social problems, but rather to pathological adherence to pre-existing frameworks for understanding the world, and to a corresponding splintering into antagonistic groups. Projection, in which, as we saw, 'the world becomes the impotent or omnipotent incarnation of what is projected onto it' (GS 3 p. 216), is amplified by the way information is channelled via the web. People stay in the echo chambers that reflect their prejudices, which are reinforced by privately owned media concerns. Talk of 'stupidity' here may seem inappropriate, but Adorno sees stupidity in terms of the systemic factors which destroy 'courage' in thinking: 'Most stupidity in thinking forms where that courage, which is immanent in thought and continually stirs in it, was stifled. Stupidity is ... not the simple absence of the power of thought, but rather the scar of its mutilation' (GS 10.2 pp. 604–5). Adorno's work is an attempt to understand the 'mutilation' of the power of thought by the systemic pressures of modern social forms, and to discover how the scar it leaves might be healed.

What primarily obstructs such healing is the fact that: 'the reproduction of stupidity, which previously took place unconsciously, under the dictates of the bare necessity of life, is, because it could be abolished, taken in hand by triumphant mass-culture' (GS 10.1 p. 101). He often underestimates what may resist 'stupidity', but the pressure of mass-culture has in certain respects actually grown in the years since his death. The increased flow of information does not lead to resistance to conformism, but often to a conformism that presents itself as resistance to conformism, which bolsters the status quo even more effectively. Clearly, just adding to the flow of information cannot counter what is at issue here, and Adorno does not claim to offer a general recipe for overcoming such systemic problems. There is, for him, no pre-existing theoretical map that will secure the direction of an investigation. This is why one has to be careful when seeking to translate his theories into contemporary practice. For all his engagement with political issues, Adorno is not an essentially political thinker who offers strategies for realizing the changes to which his ideas may point.

Adorno's major contribution lies rather in his offering models for interpreting social and cultural phenomena, in which detailed empirical investigation is complemented by the revelation of the often hidden systemic roots of those phenomena. His use of resources from Marxism, psychoanalysis, and other perspectives suggests why he does not propose any kind of systematic method. The boundaries between psychological, philosophical, economic, political, aesthetic, and sociological explanation are perennially contested. Instead of focusing on possible sceptical consequences of this situation, Adorno uses the tensions between the forms of explanation to reveal what may be missing in each when investigating real world cases. This is why he insists on 'unrestricted experience', and on 'negative dialectics'.

Negative dialectics, as we saw, does not seek to resolve the opposition between thought and its object philosophically, in the manner of Hegel. It is instead 'the consistent awareness of non-identity', of how concept and object never fully coincide, and 'does not pre-emptively adopt a standpoint' (GS 6 p. 18). In consequence—and this helps explain the resistance Adorno's work encounters, particularly among philosophers—it can have the effect of 'inducing vertigo. For the great literature of modernity since Baudelaire that feeling is central; philosophy is anachronistically told it is not permitted to have anything to do with anything of the kind' (GS 6 p. 42). The demand for 'a frame of reference, in which everything finds its place' (GS 6 p. 43) contrasts with the idea that 'Dialectic is the attempt to see the new in the old, instead of just the old in the new' (GS 5 p. 46). Philosophy has to renounce any attempt at final systematic comprehension: even the old is never fully comprehended. The alternative—which still is the norm in certain kinds of analytical philosophy today—is to aim at a definitive theory of what is being investigated. Adorno regards this as philosophy 'limiting itself to the methodology of the sciences, declaring these as philosophy, and virtually deleting itself' (GS 6 p. 20). It is not that Adorno in any way questions the general validity of modern science: 'Certainly not the last among the overdue tasks of philosophy is, without amateurish analogies and syntheses, for mind to adopt the experiences of the natural sciences' (GS 10.2 p. 470). But that is a socio-cultural task, which precisely eludes the methodology of the sciences themselves, and demands a different kind of stance, that is open to other kinds of experience, including aesthetic experience.

Adorno's Benjamin-influenced desire to establish philosophy's autonomy from scientific method means he does not see metaphysics as being concerned with 'what fundamental kinds of things there are and what properties and relations they have'. The fact is that the sciences do a better job of this than armchair philosophers. Adorno's reflections on subject and object are, unlike a lot of modern philosophy, not concerned with scepticism about cognition, but rather with the distorted relationships of the subject to the world in modernity. The questions here are 'metaphysical' because they concern how we make sense after theological and systematic metaphysical forms of meaning have been emptied out by the advances of the sciences, and by the Holocaust. Adorno, as we have seen, associates the failures of previous forms of philosophy with the idea that modern humankind's relationship to the world has become primarily one of domination, which damages both human and non-human nature. At the same time, philosophy, as a form of mind/spirit, cannot simply be superseded: 'As little as mind is the absolute is it absorbed by what there is. It will only recognise what there is if it does not abolish itself' (GS 10.2 p. 471). The task is rather for philosophy to keep open the possibility of new ways of understanding and responding to a world that is prey to systemic delusion.

This may sound rather vague, but what Adorno means becomes clearer if, rather than seeing the cognitive stance as the primary way we relate to the world, we also think in terms of doing justice to things—which suggests why art is so central to his thought.

These contrasting stances are exemplified in the way that 'nature' is that which is technologically dominated in the name of human self-preservation, but now also that which needs our protection. Adorno sums up his approach to 'non-identity' as follows: 'Reciprocal criticism of universal and particular, acts of identification which judge whether the concept does justice to what is grasped, and whether the particular also fulfils its concept, are the medium of thinking of the non-identity of particular and concept' (GS 6 p. 149). This two-way critical approach is illustrated, for example, in ways of thinking about people which stereotype them, so not doing justice to their individuality, and, in contrast, in the ways in which individuals can take themselves to be self-determining subjects when they are actually objects of their externally imposed super-ego.

The focus on the negative which runs through Adorno's work might seem to locate him as an existentialist thinker who sees humankind as faced with a meaningless universe. Such an interpretation would, though, ignore the thoroughgoing historicization upon which he insists. The world that can now appear meaningless is one which perpetuates deprivation and suffering, and abuses non-human nature in ways that it is in the power of humankind to change. As such, 'despair is the last ideology', because it is actually 'historically and socially determined' (GS 6 p. 366). The point is that appropriate social and political changes would also alter how the world manifests itself in philosophy. Negative dialectics consequently rejects both totalizing assertions of the meaningfulness of existence, and totalizing assertions of its meaninglessness: 'What would without ignominy have a claim to the name of meaning resides in what is open, not enclosed within itself; the thesis that life has none is, as a positive thesis, just as foolish as its opposite is false' (GS 6 p. 370). Traditional metaphysical assertions about the meaning of life can actually empty individual lives of meaning, because the assertions entail finality, when meaning can reside precisely in resistance to finality. Adorno speaks of truth, particularly in art, as having a 'temporal core': it may not be timeless, but that does not erase its role in making sense in particular historical circumstances.

The task is, therefore, to keep open possibilities of new meaning, at the same time as coming to terms with the end of traditional metaphysics. Adorno regards art as essential to this: 'What is said by finite beings about transcendence is its semblance [*Schein*], but, as Kant realized, a necessary semblance. That is why the salvaging [*Rettung*] of semblance, the object of aesthetics, is incomparably relevant to metaphysics' (GS 6 p. 386). What Adorno means is exemplified when he claims that Mahler's *Song of the Earth*—a piece of 'semblance'—both acknowledges and transcends the realization, brought about by the disenchantment of nature, that the earth is now one insignificant planet revolving round a minor star in one of billions of galaxies: 'The moment of rapture in the face of such beauty presumes to stand up against being beholden to disenchanted nature. That metaphysics is no longer possible becomes the last metaphysics' (GS 13 p. 297). Announcing the end of metaphysics is itself metaphysical, because it makes a universal claim. Art is, though, 'judgementless', and this means that the apparent contradiction in the announcement is obviated by the fact that the last metaphysics is manifested in the form of Mahler's music, rather than in discursive form. The semblance of transcendence may be all that remains, but art in modernity can still play a vital role in keeping us open to things to which we might otherwise be blind.

Even though redemptive theology and metaphysics disintegrate in face of the Holocaust, Adorno's approach to modern culture takes seriously the needs which they represent, needs which, as the contemporary world continues to demonstrate, can lead to destructive, irrational responses. In a world where technological command has developed well beyond what was possible even in Adorno's day, but where, in many areas, this has not been accompanied by an equivalent moral advance, a warning from

8. Adorno memorial in Frankfurt am Main.

'Education after Auschwitz' suggests why his thought is unlikely to become redundant in the foreseeable future:

> Millions of innocent people—giving the figures, let alone haggling about them is already inhuman—were systematically murdered. No living person can dismiss this as a surface phenomenon, as an aberration from the course of history which would not come into consideration in relation to the great tendency of progress, of enlightenment, of supposedly advancing humanity. (GS 10.2. p. 675)

How to advance humanity, if we take seriously what it has been shown to be capable of, is the challenge which Adorno's work still poses for us today (Figure 8).

References

Chapter 1: Life and times

References to Adorno, T. W. *Gesammelte Schriften*, 20 Volumes (Frankfurt: Suhrkamp, 1997) are to GS with the volume number. This is the standard German edition. This is gradually being supplemented by publication of transcripts of Adorno's lectures and other material (where there is an English translation of these I add the title to the reference after the German text, and the full details of the translation are given in Further Reading). All translations are my own.

Adorno, T. W. *Aspekte des neuen Rechtsradikalismus* (Frankfurt: Suhrkamp, 2019), p. 23 (English: *Aspects of the New Right-Wing Extremism*) for the 'constellation of rational means' quote.

Adorno, T. W. 'Einleitung in die Philosophie', unpublished lectures, Adorno Archiv, Akademie der Künste, Berlin (1959–60), p. 4793.

I have offered a more detailed account of Adorno, locating him in relation to contemporary philosophical debates, in Bowie 2013 (see Further Reading).

Chapter 2: The modern subject

Adorno, T. W. *Kants 'Kritik der reinen Vernunft'* (Frankfurt: Suhrkamp, 1995) (English: *Kant's 'Critique of Pure Reason'*) for the 'depth of a philosophy' (p. 128), 'behind the most abstract concepts' (p. 13), 'power' (p. 17), 'timeless truth' (p. 41), 'origin in nature' (p. 118), 'philosophy of identity' (p. 105), and 'objective meaning' (p. 168) quotes.

Francis Bacon n.d. *The Complete Works* (Centaur Classics), Kindle Locations, 7185–6.

Adorno, T. W. 'Einleitung in die Philosophie', unpublished lectures, Adorno Archiv, Akademie der Künste, Berlin (1959–60), for the 'tension' (p. 4930), 'autonomous' (p. 4893), and 'impotence of spirit' (p. 5061) quotes.

Spinoza, B. *Treatise on the Emendation of the Intellect*, published 1677.

Adorno, T. W. *Einführung in die Dialektik* (Frankfurt: Suhrkamp, 2010), p. 149 (English: *An Introduction to Dialectics*) for the 'no such last thing' quote.

Adorno, T. W. *Zur Lehre von der Geschichte und der Freiheit* (Frankfurt: Suhrkamp, 2001), p. 62 (English: *History and Freedom*) for the 'reasonableness of history' quote.

Chapter 3: Nature and history

Adorno, T. W. *Kranichsteiner Vorlesungen* (Frankfurt: Suhrkamp, 2014), p. 267 (English: *The New Music: Kranichstein Lectures*) for the 'definitions' quote.

Weber, M. 'Science as a Vocation', in Weber, M. *The Vocation Lectures* (Indianapolis, Cambridge: Hackett, 2004).

Benjamin, W. *Gesammelte Schriften* (Frankfurt: Suhrkamp, 1980), 1.2 p. 696.

Adorno, T. W. *Philosophische Elemente einer Theorie der Gesellschaft* (Frankfurt: Suhrkamp, 2008), p. 104 (English: *Philosophical Elements of a Theory of Society*).

Adorno, T. W. *Einführung in die Dialektik* (Frankfurt: Suhrkamp, 2010) for the 'no construct' (pp. 80–1) and 'encounter as nature' (pp. 166–7) quotes.

Kant, I. *Prolegomena to any Future Metaphysics*, in Kant, I n.d. *Sämtliche Werke: Philosophische Schriften, Aufsätze & Biografie* (Vollständige Ausgaben) Kindle Edition Kindle Location. 14372.

Wellmer, A. 'On Spirit as a Part of Nature', *Constellations* (Vol. 16, No. 2), 2009, for the 'living nature' (p. 220) and 'history of nature (p. 222) quotes.

Adorno, T. W. *Zur Lehre von der Geschichte und der Freiheit* (Frankfurt: Suhrkamp, 2001), for the 'everything historical' (p. 179) and 'nation is not nature' (p. 156) quotes.

Adorno, T. W. *Einführung in die Dialektik* (Frankfurt: Suhrkamp, 2010), pp. 166–7.

Graeber, D. 'On the Phenomenon of Bullshit Jobs: A Work Rant' (<https://www.strike.coop/bullshit-jobs/>).

Adorno, T. W. *Probleme der Moralphilosophie* (Frankfurt: Suhrkamp, 1996), p. 154 (English: *Problems of Moral Philosophy*).

Wellmer, A. 'On Spirit as a Part of Nature', *Constellations* (Vol. 16, No. 2), 2009, pp. 220 and 222.

Chapter 4: History and freedom

Adorno, T. W. *Zur Lehre von der Geschichte und der Freiheit* (Frankfurt: Suhrkamp, 2001), for the 'historical through and through' (p. 248), 'sphere of the objective' (p. 308), 'concept of the will' (p. 267), 'theory urges freedom' (p. 272), 'free beings' (p. 282), 'freedom gets mixed up' (p. 338), 'by dint of this impulse' (p. 330), 'something merely determined' (p. 328), and 'development of consciousness' (p. 295) quotes.

Adorno, T. W. *Probleme der Moralphilosophie* (Frankfurt: Suhrkamp, 1996), for the 'complete determinism' (p. 218), 'freedom in the absolute' (p. 82), 'double difficulty' (p. 84), 'contradictory moments' (p. 108), 'incompatible with reason' (p. 108), 'absolute realisation' (p. 108), 'freedom of the whole' (pp. 261–2), 'substantiality of ethics' (p. 22), 'cannot be prophesied' (p. 224), 'things that are conscious' (p. 226), 'suffer from their knowledge' (p. 168), 'moment of irrationality' (p. 17), 'right action' (p. 144), and 'learning in reflection' (p. 251) quotes.

Adorno, T. W. *The Authoritarian Personality* (London: Verso, 2020), p. 113.

Chapter 5: The culture industry

Adorno, T. W. *Philosophische Elemente einer Theorie der Gesellschaft* (Frankfurt: Suhrkamp, 2008), p. 117.

Polanyi, K. *The Great Transformation: The Political and Economic Origins of our Time* (Boston: Beacon. Kindle edition, 2001), p. 44.

Adorno, T. W. *Zur Theorie der musikalischen Reproduktion* (Frankfurt: Suhrkamp, 2001), p. 172 (English: *Towards a Theory of Musical Reproduction*) for the 'light falls' quote.

Chapter 6: Society

The Independent 17 November 2020 <https://www.independent. co.uk/news/world/americas/covid-us-cases-latest-nurse-patients- biden-virus-b1724026.html?fbclid=IwAR1ZNsO1-nhDq5f8_ EbdIKVjzIDOA3CKvFHdpI0QQOfIagBhy0Iu2kamnn Q>.

Adorno, T. W. *Philosophische Elemente einer Theorie der Gesellschaft* (Frankfurt: Suhrkamp, 2008), for the 'object domains' (p. 140), 'lacking in qualities' (p. 28), 'no coincidence' (p. 44), 'advanced age' (p. 30), and 'becomes its own opposite' (p. 47) quotes.

Vox 13 November 2020 <https://www.vox.com/future-perfect/ 21561066/covid-19-mink-mutation-denmark-cull>.

Price, H. 'Truth as Convenient Friction', *The Journal of Philosophy* (Vol. 100, No. 4) Apr. 2003, p. 170.

Putnam, H. *The Collapse of the Fact/Value Dichotomy and Other Essays* (Cambridge, Mass.: Harvard University Press, 2004), pp. 142, 145.

Adorno, T. W. 'Fragen der Dialektik', unpublished lectures, Adorno Archiv, Akademie der Künste, Berlin, 1963–4, p. 9056 for the 'measure of comparability' quote.

Adorno, T. W. *Probleme der Moralphilosophie* (Frankfurt: Suhrkamp, 1996), p. 131 for the 'reason which makes itself independent' quote.

Chapter 7: Art and philosophy

Sellars: in Colodny, R. (ed.) *Science, Perception, and Reality* (Ridgeview: Humanities Press, 1962), p. 35.

Adorno, T. W. *Ontologie und Dialektik* (Frankfurt: Suhrkamp, 2002), p. 236 (English: *Ontology and Dialectics*) for the 'aesthetic impossibility' quote.

Adorno, T. W. 'Ästhetik', unpublished lectures, Adorno Archiv, Akademie der Künste, Berlin (1961), p. 6467 for the 'self-consciousness of the epoch' quote.

Barenboim, D. and Said, E. *Parallels and Paradoxes* (London: Bloomsbury, 2004), p. 122.

Schönberg, A. *Style and Idea* (New York: St Martins Press, 1975), p. 217.

Adorno, T. W. *Vorträge 1949–1968* (Frankfurt: Suhrkamp, 2019), p. 106.

Bowie, A. *Music, Philosophy, and Modernity* (Cambridge: Cambridge University Press, 2007), ch. 9 re 'philosophical music'.

Wellmer, A. *Zur Dialektik von Moderne und Postmoderne* (Frankfurt: Suhrkamp, 1985), p. 29.

Chapter 8: Doing justice to things

Williamson, T. *The Philosophy of Philosophy* (Oxford: Oxford University Press, 2007), p. 19.

Bowie, A. *Aesthetic Dimensions of Modern Philosophy* (Oxford: Oxford University Press 2022), re world in modernity.

Further reading

These are the main translations of Adorno's work: (GS and a number refers to the volume number of the *Gesammelte Schriften* from which the translation is taken). It is probably best to begin by reading his lectures, as these are generally more accessible than the texts written for publication.

Aesthetics (Lectures 1958–9), trans. W. Hoban (Cambridge: Polity, 2006).

Aesthetic Theory (1970), trans. R. Hullot-Kentor (Minneapolis: University of Minnesota Press, 1997) (GS 7).

Against Epistemology: A Metacritique; Studies in Husserl and the Phenomenological Antinomies (1956), trans. W. Domingo (Cambridge, Mass.: MIT Press, 1982) (GS 5).

An Introduction to Dialectics (Lectures 1958) (Cambridge: Polity, 2017).

Aspects of the New Right-Wing Extremism (1967), trans. W. Hoban (Cambridge: Polity, 2020).

The Authoritarian Personality, T. W. Adorno et al. (New York: Harper & Brothers, 1950) (GS 9.1).

Alban Berg: Master of the Smallest Link (1968), trans. J. Brand and C. Hailey (Cambridge: Cambridge University Press, 1991) (GS 13).

Beethoven: The Philosophy of Music; Fragments and Texts (1993), ed. R. Tiedemann, trans. E. Jephcott (Cambridge: Polity Press, 1998).

Critical Models: Interventions and Catchwords (1963, 1969), trans. H. W. Pickford (New York: Columbia University Press, 1998) (GS 10.2).

Dialectic of Enlightenment: Philosophical Fragments (1947),
M. Horkheimer and T. W. Adorno, ed. G. S. Noerr, trans. E. Jephcott
(Stanford, Calif.: Stanford University Press, 2002) (GS 3).

Hegel: Three Studies (1963), trans. S. Weber Nicholsen (Cambridge,
Mass.: MIT Press, 1993) (GS 5).

History and Freedom (Lectures 1964–1965), trans. R. Livingstone
(Cambridge: Polity, 2006).

In Search of Wagner (1952), trans. R. Livingstone (London: NLB,
1981) (GS 13).

Introduction to Sociology (1968), trans. E. Jephcott (Cambridge:
Polity, 1999).

The Jargon of Authenticity (1964), trans. K. Tarnowski and F. Will
(London: Routledge & Kegan Paul, 1973) (GS 6).

Kant's Critique of Pure Reason (Lectures 1959), ed. R. Tiedemann,
trans. R. Livingstone (Cambridge: Polity, 2006).

Kierkegaard: Construction of the Aesthetic (1933), trans.
R. Hullot-Kentor (Minneapolis: University of Minnesota
Press, 1989) (GS 2).

*Lectures on Negative Dialectics: Fragments of a Lecture Course
1965/1966*, ed. R. Tiedemann, trans. R. Livingstone (Cambridge:
Polity, 2008).

Mahler: A Musical Physiognomy (1960), trans. E. Jephcott (Chicago:
University of Chicago Press, 1988) (GS 13).

Metaphysics: Concept and Problems (Lectures 1965), ed.
R. Tiedemann, trans. E. Jephcott (Cambridge: Polity, 2001).

Minima Moralia: Reflections from Damaged Life (1951), trans.
E. F. N. Jephcott (London: NLB, 1974) (GS 4).

Negative Dialectics (1966), trans. E. B. Ashton (New York: Seabury
Press, 1973) (GS 6).

Notes to Literature (1958, 1961, 1965, 1974), 2 vols., ed. R. Tiedemann,
trans. S. Weber Nicholsen (New York: Columbia University Press,
1991, 1992) (GS 11).

Ontology and Dialectics (Lectures 1960–1), trans. N. Walker
(Cambridge: Polity, 2019).

Prisms (1955), trans. S. Weber and S. Weber (Cambridge, Mass.: MIT
Press, 1981 (GS 10.1).

Philosophical Elements of a Theory of Society (Lectures 1964), trans.
W. Hoban (Cambridge: Polity, 2019).

Philosophy of New Music (1949), trans., ed., and with an introduction
by R. Hullot-Kentor (Minneapolis: University of Minnesota Press,
2006) (GS 12).

Problems of Moral Philosophy (Lectures 1963), ed. T. Schröder, trans.
R. Livingstone (Cambridge: Polity, 1999).

The Positivist Dispute in German Sociology (1969), T. W. Adorno,
et al., trans. G. Adey and D. Frisby (London: Heinemann,
1976) (GS 8).

The New Music: Kranichstein Lectures, trans. W. Hoban (Cambridge:
Polity 2021).

Towards a Theory of Musical Reproduction (2001), trans. W. Hoban
(Cambridge: Polity, 2006).

Adorno Anthologies

The Adorno Reader, ed. B. O'Connor (Oxford: Blackwell, 2000).

Can One Live after Auschwitz? A Philosophical Reader, ed.
R. Tiedemann, trans. R. Livingstone et al. (Stanford, Calif.:
Stanford University Press, 2003).

The Culture Industry: Selected Essays on Mass Culture, ed.
J. M. Bernstein (London: Routledge, 1991).

Essays on Music: Theodor W. Adorno, ed. R. D. Leppert, trans.
S. H. Gillespie et al. (Berkeley: University of California
Press, 2002).

Selected secondary reading

Benhabib, S. *Critique, Norm, and Utopia: A Study of the Foundations
of Critical Theory* (New York: Colombia University Press, 1986).

Benzer, M. *The Sociology of Theodor Adorno* (Cambridge: Cambridge
University Press, 2011).

Bernstein, J. M. *Adorno: Disenchantment and Ethics* (Cambridge:
Cambridge University Press, 2001).

Bernstein, J. M. (ed.), *Art and Aesthetics after Adorno* (Cambridge:
Cambridge University Press, 2010).

Bowie, A. *From Romanticism to Critical Theory* (London:
Routledge, 1997).

Bowie, A. *Adorno and the Ends of Philosophy* (Cambridge:
Polity, 2013).

Brunkhorst, H. *Adorno and Critical Theory* (Cardiff: University of
Wales Press, 1999).

Buck-Morss, S. *The Origin of Negative Dialectics; Theodor W. Adorno,
Walter Benjamin and the Frankfurt Institute* (New York: Free
Press, 1977).

Claussen, D. Theodor W. *Adorno: One Last Genius*, trans. R. Livingstone (Cambridge, Mass.: Harvard University Press, 2008).

Cook, D. *Adorno on Nature* (Durham: Acumen, 2011).

Foster, R. *Adorno: The Recovery of Experience* (Albany, NY: State University of New York Press, 2007).

Freyenhagen, F. *Adorno's Practical Philosophy: Living Less Wrongly* (Cambridge: Cambridge University Press, 2013).

Gibson, N. C., and A. Rubin (eds) *Adorno: A Critical Reader* (Oxford: Blackwell, 2002).

Gordon, P. E. *Adorno and Existence* (Cambridge, Mass.: Harvard University Press, 2016).

Gordon, P. E., Hammer, E, Pensky, M. (eds) *A Companion to Adorno* (Oxford: Blackwell, 2020).

Hammer, E. *Adorno and the Political* (New York: Routledge, 2006).

Hammer, E. *Adorno's Modernism: Art, Experience, and Catastrophe* (Cambridge: Cambridge University Press, 2015).

Heberle, R. J. (ed.), *Feminist Interpretations of Theodor Adorno* (University Park, Pa: Pennsylvania State University Press, 2006).

Hohendahl, P. U. *Prismatic Thought: Theodor W. Adorno* (Lincoln, Nebr.: University of Nebraska Press, 1995).

Hohendahl, P. U. *The Fleeting Promise of Art: Adorno's Aesthetic Theory Revisited* (Ithaca, NY: Cornell University Press, 2013).

Honneth, A. *Pathologies of Reason: On the Legacy of Critical Theory*, trans. J. Ingram et al. (New York: Columbia University Press, 2009).

Huhn, T. (ed.) *The Cambridge Companion to Adorno* (Cambridge: Cambridge University Press, 2004).

Huhn, T., and L. Zuidervaart (eds) *The Semblance of Subjectivity: Essays in Adorno's Aesthetic Theory* (Cambridge, Mass.: MIT Press, 1997).

Jameson, F. *Late Marxism: Adorno, or, The Persistence of the Dialectic* (London: Verso, 1990).

Jarvis, S. *Adorno: A Critical Introduction* (London: Routledge, 1998).

Jarvis, S. (ed.) *Theodor Adorno* 4 vols (London: Routledge, 2006).

Jay, M. *Adorno* (London: Fontana, 1984).

Jay, M. *The Dialectical Imagination* 2nd edn (Berkeley: University of California Press, 1996).

Müller-Doohm, S. *Adorno: A Biography*, trans. R. Livingstone (Cambridge: Polity Press, 2005).

Nicholsen, S. W. *Exact Imagination, Late Work: On Adorno's Aesthetics* (Cambridge, Mass.: MIT Press, 1997).

O'Connor, B. *Adorno's Negative Dialectic: Philosophy and the Possibility of Critical Rationality* (Cambridge, Mass.: MIT Press, 2004).

O'Connor, B. *Adorno* (London: Routledge, 2013).

Okiji, F. *Jazz as Critique: Adorno and Black Expression Revisited* (Stanford, Calif.: Stanford University Press, 2018).

Paddison, M. *Adorno's Aesthetics of Music* (Cambridge: Cambridge University Press, 1993).

Rose, G. *The Melancholy Science: An Introduction to the Thought of Theodor W. Adorno* (London: Macmillan Press, 1978).

Shuster, M. *Autonomy after Auschwitz: Adorno, German Idealism, and Modernity* (Chicago: The University of Chicago Press, 2014).

Wiggershaus, R. *The Frankfurt School: Its History, Theories, and Political Significance* trans. M. Robertson (Cambridge, Mass.: MIT Press, 1994).

Wilson, R. *Adorno* (London: Routledge, 2008).

Zuidervaart, L. *Adorno's Aesthetic Theory: The Redemption of Illusion* (Cambridge, Mass.: MIT Press, 1991).

Zuidervaart, L. *Social Philosophy after Adorno* (Cambridge: Cambridge University Press, 2007).

Index

A

aesthetic, aesthetics 10, 36, 56, 62, 85–103
anti-Semitism 7, 14, 82
art 4, 7, 10, 28, 29, 35, 36, 62–4, 85–103, 108, 110
  and politics 91, 93
  and truth 88, 109
Arendt, H. 9

B

Beckett, S. 101
Beethoven, L. van 86, 88, 89, 96–7
Benjamin, W. 4, 28, 91

C

capitalism 45, 54, 58, 89
  neoliberal 1–2, 59, 77, 105
categorical imperative 49
  new 50–1
conformism 3, 42, 52, 55–6, 58, 59, 64, 79, 105–6
contradiction 12, 41, 47, 73–4
Covid-19 31, 67–8, 72–3, 80
culture industry 53–64, 106

D

delusion 14, 29, 45, 53–5, 62, 66, 78, 79, 82, 93, 105, 108
dialectic, dialectical 11–12, 18, 20, 31–2, 34, 44, 60, 71, 72, 95, 99–100, 107
  negative 29, 107, 109

E

Enlightenment 11–12, 42, 57
ethics and moral philosophy 46–52
exaggeration 53–4, 66

F

fascism 3, 9, 65, 69, 78, 81
Flaubert, G. 104
freedom 16, 24, 30, 37, 38–52, 79, 90, 91–6
  of the will 38–40, 44, 47
Freud, S. 6, 68–9, 78

G

German Idealism 20, 86

H

Habermas, J. 83
Hegel, G. W. F. 11, 20–4, 25, 26, 29, 37, 45, 48, 66, 75, 86, 96, 97, 107
history 27–37, 38–52
Holocaust (Auschwitz) 7, 28, 39, 45, 50–1, 66, 78–9, 108, 111
Hume, D. 17–18

I

identity 15, 19, 21
  non-identity 19, 107, 108
ideology 23, 40, 58, 109

J

jazz 54, 59–64

K

Kant, I. 14–20, 25, 30, 40–1, 49–50

L

law 23–4, 45, 84
Lukács, G. 4

M

Mahler, G. 90, 102, 104, 110
Mann, T. 90
Marx, K. 3, 6, 19, 23, 25, 57
  and Engels 31
metaphysics 27–8, 87, 92, 101, 108, 110
mimesis 35–7, 94–5, 99
modernism (avant-garde) 87, 88, 93–4, 101

music 57, 62–3, 88, 90, 92, 93, 94, 95–100
mythology 14

N

nationalism 32, 59
nature 13, 19, 20, 27–37, 48–9, 73, 99–100, 108–9, 110
  second 32–4, 92, 95
Nazism 7–8, 24, 79, 82, 86
neuroscience 33–4
Nietzsche, F. 6, 12–13, 90, 97

P

philosophy 3, 12, 16, 17, 22–3, 29, 37, 44–5, 85–6, 88–9, 98–9, 104, 107–8
Polanyi, K. 58
Popper, K. 65, 71–4
'Positivism Dispute in German Sociology' 4, 65–77
Price, H. 75
projection 13–14, 45–6, 62, 78, 81–2, 105–6
psychoanalysis 13–14, 18–19, 41–2, 49, 68–9, 78
Putnam, H. 75

R

racism 33, 45, 78, 105
reason 12, 42, 74, 83
  instrumental 13, 34, 41–2, 73, 83
reification 71, 76

S

Schoenberg, A. 6, 87, 88, 97–8, 100, 104

science 14, 16, 28, 65–70, 107–8
  scientism 70–72
Second Viennese School
  96, 99
sociology 65–77, 82
Stravinsky, I. 99
student movement 2–3, 8–9
subject 11–26, 33–4, 36, 43–6, 49,
  50, 51, 64, 68, 70–1, 79, 95–6,
  108, 109

T

theory 2, 44, 46–7, 64, 65–70
  critical 71–5

W

Wagner, R. 97
Weber, M. 6, 28, 67, 83
Wellmer, A. 30–1, 37, 101–2

German Philosophy
A Very Short Introduction
Andrew Bowie

German Philosophy: A Very Short Introduction discusses the idea that German philosophy forms one of the most revealing responses to the problems of 'modernity'. The rise of the modern natural sciences and the related decline of religion raises a series of questions, which recur throughout German philosophy, concerning the relationships between knowledge and faith, reason and emotion, and scientific, ethical, and artistic ways of seeing the world. There are also many significant philosophers who are generally neglected in most existing English-language treatments of German philosophy, which tend to concentrate on the canonical figures. This *Very Short Introduction* will include reference to these thinkers and suggests how they can be used to question more familiar German philosophical thought.

GERMAN LITERATURE
A Very Short Introduction
Nicholas Boyle

German writers, from Luther and Goethe to Heine, Brecht, and Günter Grass, have had a profound influence on the modern world. This *Very Short Introduction* presents an engrossing tour of the course of German literature from the late Middle Ages to the present, focussing especially on the last 250 years. Emphasizing the economic and religious context of many masterpieces of German literature, it highlights how they can be interpreted as responses to social and political changes within an often violent and tragic history. The result is a new and clear perspective which illuminates the power of German literature and the German intellectual tradition, and its impact on the wider cultural world.

'Boyle has a sure touch and an obvious authority...this is a balanced and lively introduction to German literature.'

Ben Hutchinson, TLS

MODERNISM
A Very Short Introduction
Christopher Butler

Whether we recognise it or not, virtually every aspect of our life today has been influenced in part by the aesthetic legacy of Modernism. In this *Very Short Introduction* Christopher Butler examines how and why Modernism began, explaining what it is and showing how it has gradually informed all aspects of 20th and 21st century life. Butler considers several aspects of modernism including some modernist works; movements and notions of the avant garde; and the idea of 'progress' in art. Butler looks at modernist ideas of the self, subjectivity, irrationalism, people and machines, and political definitions of modernism as a whole.

www.oup.com/vsi

UTOPIANISM
A Very Short Introduction
Lyman Tower Sargent

This *Very Short Introduction* explores utopianism and its history. Lyman Sargent discusses the role of utopianism in literature, and in the development of colonies and in immigration. The idea of utopia has become commonplace in social and political thought, both negatively and positively. Some thinkers see a trajectory from utopia to totalitarianism with violence an inevitable part of the mix. Others see utopia directly connected to freedom and as a necessary element in the fight against totalitarianism. In Christianity utopia is labelled as both heretical and as a fundamental part of Christian belief, and such debates are also central to such fields as architecture, town and city planning, and sociology among many others.

www.oup.com/vsi

EXISTENTIALISM
A Very Short Introduction
Thomas Flynn

Existentialism was one of the leading philosophical movements of the twentieth century. Focusing on its seven leading figures, Sartre, Nietzsche, Heidegger, Kierkegaard, de Beauvoir, Merleau-Ponty and Camus, this *Very Short Introduction* provides a clear account of the key themes of the movement which emphasized individuality, free will, and personal responsibility in the modern world. Drawing in the movement's varied relationships with the arts, humanism, and politics, this book clarifies the philosophy and original meaning of 'existentialism' - which has tended to be obscured by misappropriation. Placing it in its historical context, Thomas Flynn also highlights how existentialism is still relevant to us today.

www.oup.com/vsi